THE TRANSFORMATIVE POWER OF A NAME

Incredible Accounts of Eleven Women Determined to Discover and Unleash Their Unique Identities

by Visionary Author:
Cecily Cooper

with Co-Authors:
Shannon Walker, Dr. Judine Berlus, Dianne Reid, Sophia K. Tade, Brittani Wegner, Kem S. Kitchen, Dr. Griselda T. Martinez, Felicity Blunt, MA, LPC-S, NCC, Ravonda B. Oden, Erika D. Gould Brown

Foreword written by:
Bishop Wayne Malcolm, The Business Bishop

Published by iBounceback Greater, LLC
P.O. Box 645
Ellicott City, MD 21041
www.bouncebackgreater.com
bouncebackgreatercoaching@gmail.com

Cover Design by: Saiqa Falak

ISBN: 979-8-9894577-0-0
Printed in the United States of America

THE TRANSFORMATIVE POWER OF A NAME

CONTENTS

Dedication

Foreword

Acknowledgments

From Ignored to Heard: The Birth of Chinasa

Cecily Cooper ______ *06*

Mom

Shannon Walker ______ *19*

I Am Chosen: From Rejected to Appointed

Dr. Judine Berlus ______ *28*

Daughter

Dianne Reid ______ *38*

Embracing the Promises of Kikeloman (Kee-keh-lohman)

Sophia K. Tade ______ *47*

What's in a Name

Brittani Wegner ______ *56*

Rejected to Redeemed: One of God's Chosen

Kem S. Kitchen ______ *65*

A Daughter Redeemed Her Name

Dr. Griselda T. Martínez ______ *75*

Becoming Happiness

Felicity Blunt, MA, LPC S, NCC ______ *84*

Defining Me

Ravonda B. Oden ______ *94*

The Birth and End of Romantic Woman

Erika D. Gould Brown ______ *102*

ABOUT THE AUTHORS

CECILY COOPER 111

SHANNON WALKER 112

DR. JUDINE BERLUS 113

DIANNE REID 114

SOPHIA K. TADE 115

BRITTANI WEGNER 116

KEM S. KITCHEN 117

DR. GRISELDA MARTÍNEZ 118

FELICITY BLUNT, MA, LPC-S, NCC 119

RAVONDA B. ODEN 120

ERIKA D. GOULD BROWN 121

DEDICATION

I would like to dedicate this book to my line sister, Michelle Diane Johnson. Back in 1988, upon our initiation into Delta Sigma Theta Sorority, Inc., Michelle was gifted with the name "Endurance." As a young black woman, she possessed exceptional resilience, enduring numerous challenges with remarkable fortitude. Michelle transitioned from earth on April 10, 2023 just before this book project began. She will be deeply missed, and forever loved, by my fellow line sisters, who together formed our line known as "Jahili"--women of courage and bravery.

Richard Bach, an American writer, once said, "What the caterpillar calls the end of the world, the master calls a butterfly." Therefore, this book is also a heartfelt tribute to the young girl within every reader who may not have realized her unique worth. May the beautiful stories within this body of work inspire you to recognize and accept the divine purpose assigned to your life. May each God-inspired narrative signal the end of your weeping season and the ushering in of joyous new ones. (Psalm 30:5)

FOREWORD

Names, in many respects, represent 'frames' in which people are either limited or liberated to realize their innate potential. This is why God changed the names of some of the patriarchs of Israel, before changing their circumstances. Perhaps the Scriptures were revealing a profound psychological truth, i.e. that we never truly change our lives until we successfully change our self-image.

Meaningful change is always an inside job. The real work begins when we question our own assumptions and begin doubting the descriptions that others gave to us. It involves a journey of self-discovery in which we locate and unleash our authentic self. It then takes courage, conviction and character to stand up, to stand out and to stand tall, in the face of criticism, jealousy and envy. But only when you do give volume to your own voice and expression to your true essence, can you inspire, equip and enable others to break free from the frames and names that stifle creativity, authenticity and transformation.

I pray that these stories, that are beautifully curated by Cecily Cooper, serve to inspire and empower your own reformation and ultimate revelation.

Bishop Wayne Malcolm
The Business Bishop

ACKNOWLEDGMENTS

To my Lord and Savior Jesus Christ: Your Love has transformed the details of my life. Thank You!

I am eternally grateful for my mentor, Pastor/Dr. Dharius Daniels, First Lady Shameka Daniels and the entire i3/TCP staff and team. "PD", as he is affectionately called by those who know and love him, has singlehandedly transformed my life by addressing my most debilitating limited beliefs and then coaching me beyond them. Without his anointed teachings, his highly skilled and caring staff and the life-changing live trainings, my dreams may never have been restored to life. Because of his dedication to the call of God on his life, life has been breathed back into the "dry bones" of my life…that they might THRIVE.

I also want to express gratitude towards my Coach, Bishop Wayne Malcolm, the Business Bishop. His impactful Kingdom-focused trainings have awakened a hunger in me to live from the position of dominion… instead of defeat. Thank you for your support, Bishop!

I also owe a great deal of gratitude to the amazing cohort of i3/TCP entrepreneurs that I have met over the last eighteen months. There are just too many of you amazing individuals to name! However, special acknowledgments must be given to my friend, Jacqueline B. Grice, Founder of Launching Deeper. For her willingness to live courageously and transparently, I am eternally grateful. Thank you for affirming the God in me! I would also like to thank Lance Williams and Dr. Bettina Solawzi for being supportive members of the "tribe with my vibe."

I am also happy and grateful for my biological family. My chapter was shared in the hopes that walls would give way to bridges. May the Light of Christ illuminate the darkness so that the Son might shine in.

To Kelvin Oden, the amazingly talented artist that believed in my vision. Thank you!

To the ten brave women who trusted me enough to start and finish this journey with me, I will always thank God for your trust and for your willingness to be "the one" who God could trust with this beautiful assignment. May God bless you with a double portion of His strength and grace. May your pain give way to purpose that brings 1 Corinthians 2:9 into your full view. May His Love for each of you cause the banner "beautifully morphed" to be forever over your lovely heads.

Lastly, to everyone who inspired me to keep going, I thank you from the bottom of my heart. God knows who are you…and I will never forget your loving support of this project.

REFLECTIONS

FROM IGNORED TO HEARD: THE BIRTH OF CHINASA

CECILY COOPER

During a once-in-a-lifetime *Door of Return,* Nigerian excursion, I awaited my chance to dip my finger in the symbolic food. It was presented to those participating in a powerful name-changing ceremony; I listened in awe to the beautiful rechristening being given to each of my travel companions. The little girl within me felt like I was back in line, biding time until it was my turn to hop on Black Santa's lap and tell him what I wanted. My innerchild wanted a *beautiful* banner to hang over my head to replace those that acted as toxic synonyms for the one that always seemed to frame my existence: *unwanted.* When the moment arrived for my baptism into a new nomenclature, I braced myself to be underwhelmed so as not to experience the disappointment that always seemed to be my portion. Yet, within the inner chambers of my soul, I secretly nurtured the hope that it was finally my opportunity to truly experience uniqueness. Despite all my protective walls, I allowed a mustard seed amount of faith to germinate in the soil of my heart that *this* moment would be *the* moment when everything changed for the better.

Cecily. Be honest with yourself. What evidence do you have to believe that life would suddenly begin to offer you anything more than the usual crumbs?

This anxious inner voice in my mind was growing increasingly persuasive. I convinced myself that I just couldn't bear to have invested over five thousand dollars and endured a transatlantic journey, complete with a lengthy lay over in Dubai, only to feel betrayed by my own high hopes.

I prepared my heart to settle for having to observe and celebrate the breakthroughs of others while silently accepting that my own experience would be less than noteworthy. I recalibrated my expectations to fit my current comfort zones…where there was little to no room for growth.

Only when the entire room collectively gasped as the presenter spoke and defined my newly acquired Nigerian name did an almost imperceptible *shift* begin in my life:

Cecily Cooper! Your name is Chinasa…which means: God answers my prayers!

Wow. The holy hush in my spirit gave way to revelation: If God ANSWERS my prayers then that MUST mean that God HEARS my prayers! That moment in 2018 represented a break in the mental and emotional storm clouds that only the One Who calls me the "apple of His eye" could have arranged. THAT MOMENT was the spiritual indication that an uncoupling of my bloodline from generational curses, and a disruption in the uncelebrated trajectory of my life, had finally occurred. God had *finally* answered my heart's deepest, most desperate cry for a sense of belongingness.

But oh, how my soul looked back, and it wondered, how I got over, echoing the rhetorical inquiry of the classic Gospel song. How did I make it through the aching segments of my childhood and early adulthood years? My freshly inspired Nigerian moniker revealed these answers which can only be credited to a God Who knew what He had placed within me. Suddenly there was proof that Abba had heard me late in the midnight hour when my soul desperately cried out for acceptance, acknowledgment, and affirmation. Sadly, though, my inward sighs and lamentations often remained unnoticed by those who should have been the first to lend an ear.

Pick up the phone, pleeeease, just pick up the phone. Please. I need you.

After calling his phone and letting it ring and ring until the line would eventually result in a rapid busy signal, I convinced myself that he, the man who had been placed upon an elevated platform within my heart, didn't pick up because he was set to arrive within a matter of minutes. So, I did what every ivory-towered, imprisoned princess does as she anticipated her chivalrous knight in shining armor to rescue her from her despair–I went back to watching and eagerly expecting. While lying on the dirty mudroom floor, I could feel the cold air through my thin shirt penetrate my young bones. On my belly, I peered out of the letter-sized mail slot at the bottom of the front door. I would be there for HOURS if needed. My ears would be straining to hear the *purr* of his green Karmann Ghia Volkswagen coming to rescue me while my eyes desperately scanned back and forth within the limited view afforded by a small rectangular hole that was only meant for envelopes–not for a small pair of longing, brown eyes. That wooden opening often became my lookout post as I silently prayed: *Please don't disappoint me again. Please! I need you to come get me.* My hand to God, from blocks away, my ears could detect the approaching of that German-made engine *above every other engine*. My mind ingrained the sound into memory as I yearned for relief from various challenges: the humiliation of having to visit the local convenience store with food stamps (which often failed to cover all our needs); the upheaval of my emotional balance due to frequent relocations; the excessive discipline that followed when my chaotic environment triggered the anxiety, fear, and anger residing within me which often led to conflicts with my siblings when left unsupervised. We fought like cats and dogs, with knives being hurled at one another and with words being used that would cut deeper than any kitchen utensil ever could. Ultimately, my heart's tiny, imperceptible wounds began to add up over time and would ultimately serve as tally marks upon my nervous system. As it goes, my body began to keep meticulous score of my childhood trauma. My desperation to escape from what felt like prison was the residual effect of poverty and way too many violent slaps across my face from the hands of a single mother who was the epitome of a hustler/survivor living beyond her means but who desperately tried to do what she knew to do to keep her head above water. Her attempts to battle her demons while balancing being a primary provider left me feeling dangerously neglected. And as a result, fighting and toying with the idea of taking my own life frequently vied for my unstructured time and attention. So, yes, I willed myself to lay on that well-trodden floor, where no child belonged—and for as long as it took—until I could hear the sound of relief in the form of a VW Beetle coming to save me. After all, it was Friday, and my rescuer—my Superman—was scheduled to appear. He was supposed to make everything wrong, right. That man was my *mostly* faithful weekend dad.

And, boy, did I adore him. The smell of his cologne left me feeling intoxicated. The excitement displayed on his handsome face when he greeted me as I climbed into the backseat of his pristine car juxtaposed the clutter and sense of invisibility that surrounded me all week long. His charm, his love of the arts, and his good looks convinced me to prop my father up to the place where all absent parents seem to find themselves: celebrity status. But when my seemingly rock-star father chose his own life and freedom while overlooking the detrimental impact that everyday life was having upon me, it instilled a belief that would take years to unlearn: *self-reliance was the crucial element to survival, and vulnerability should be avoided at all cost.*

Hence, when my Superman—who had promised to pick me up at 2 p.m. that day to whisk me away from what I would describe as loneliness, depression, suffocation, rejection, abuse, and the heaviness of poverty—failed to arrive until 5 p.m. or 8 p.m. *or occasionally not at all,* I was ill-equipped to cope with the compounding effects of broken promises and "casual betrayals."

I first heard that phrase from trauma expert Patrick Teahan, who describes the term as "a situation where a person seems to care very little about acknowledging the harmful effects of letting someone down," and it immediately resonated with me. The effects of having my heart repeatedly disappointed by the one that I cherished—without so much as an apology or an explanation—left internal scars that went unaddressed for years. Realistically, had someone dared to non-judgmentally ask me, "*Why are you so angry*?" I doubt that my adolescent brain would have really known. I had never been permitted to express my thoughts on matters that weighed on my heart based upon the cultural norms within the Black community which mandated that children remain silent.

To put it plainly, I grew up feeling powerless over my circumstances. The adage *what goes on in this house STAYS in this house* strangled my voice. And to add insult to injury, I felt no real emotional connection to my mother. Due to this disconnect, nothing but pure *rage* would surge through me after being beaten by her and then forced to invalidate the shedding of my tears and the need for consolation as expressing either put me at risk of receiving additional punishment. The heaviness of my soul during these episodes of domestic violence compared side by side with daddy-daughter experiences that included: traveling annually to Disneyland, summertime trips to the beach, weekly trips to Barnes & Noble (followed by White Castle meals delivered by servers on roller-skates), painting, biking riding, rock climbing in Central Park, etc., made it difficult to *BREATHE* when I was not with my father. As time passed, the weekend experiences began to create more tension between my challenging current circumstances and the growing notion of the possibility of a life free from the constraints of perpetual hardship. Unfortunately, akin to a needle abruptly halting on a vinyl record, the weekends away would draw to a rapid close as Sunday afternoon approached. Once again, I was loaded back into his car as the feeling of being caged climbed into the backseat with me. *My mostly faithful weekend dad was ALWAYS punctual when it was time to bring me back home.*

I felt unseen. And the two people, my father and paternal grandmother, who made a way of escape—even if only for the weekend—could only do so in their limited way. My maternal grandmother, who occupied the most substantial space within my heart's inner sanctum, unexpectedly exited my life after losing a battle with lupus—a disease that I didn't even know she had until it claimed her. Her sudden death left a huge hole in my spirit that poked aggressively at my abandonment issues and left me void of real advocates. There were now only a few other places where the essence of my being could find refuge. And on those weekends when my dad would fail to show or even answer the phone to offer an explanation, the notion of being insignificant and unworthy of respect was unconsciously claimed as my truth. These feelings would be reinforced in a million different ways by the enemy of my soul until I came into absolute agreement with his lies. This would ultimately reshape my personality, usher in an orphan spirit (where I experienced a sense of not fitting in anywhere), and lead me into all kinds of self-sabotaging behaviors before the truth of God's Word set me free. And since it's true that whatever we don't understand, we will misuse, I became prone to taking for granted the people who showed me kindness while partnering with those who possessed toxic, narcissistic personalities who would come to selfishly consume the very best parts of me. These decisions revealed the impact of the deep hurt inflicted by parents who had not healed their inner child before having me. Both were lost and in need of being rescued.

By the time I reached middle school, the conflict between my mother and me grew to an unbearable point, and it was agreed upon that I should live with my father full-time. This decision was trajectory-altering because I finally had the structure, peace, and freedom I needed to stabilize; though, ultimately, I found myself totally unprepared to deal with Dad's mental health issues…alone. One would think I would have known after seeing the frustrations of the women who came and went. However, I had to learn the hard way that he could go from being a charming extrovert to a brooding recluse without warning. Sometimes, the dark side of his moody temperament might mean that I would have to sleep in the dim, dank stairwell of our apartment building, where the smell of urine and the fear of bodily harm would assume the role of tormentors because my father, my protector, would lock me out. Other times, I would endure the emotional abuse of having him refuse to speak to me—or even look at me—for *months* on end when I did something that aggravated him. This particular form of punishment was worse than my mother's physical reprimands because, by and by,

I craved a home life where connection, love, acceptance, joy, laughter, and consistent emotional and financial stability resided. So, when my father refused to speak to me, choosing instead to write his messages on a notepad or on the bathroom mirror with a bar of soap, I learned to find solace in the fact that I had a roof over my head that night.

But that was then, and this is now. From the outside, and as a grown woman, I don't look like what I've been through. Yet, beneath the shield of my protective barrier, I continue to grapple with the fear of losing something dear to me, a battle yet to be won. The residue of standing at my dad's front door, not knowing if the lock would turn within its chamber, is just beginning to loosen its hold on my sense of security. I have made adjustments, and I can now see the counter-productive patterns more clearly that show up in my relationships, from time to time, as a result of years of being ignored. I have worked to regain a sense of autonomy where I now see myself as the one who gets to create my sense of safety and peace. I am now better equipped to fight off the demonic voices that periodically come to whisper: *No one really cares about you. It would be easier if you just took some pills and laid down to die.*

The love of my praying grandmother and her warnings that anyone who takes his/her own life would go straight to hell proved enough to pull me through the darkest night terrors and seasons of spiritual warfare. I am completely convinced that my Heavenly Father chose me—INTENTIONALLY— for Himself. *I am Chinasa…and God ANSWERS my prayers.*

Truthfully speaking, however, it would take the birth of my son to get me to choose me for me! His arrival stopped me from chasing after the elusive sense of belonging from other people so that I could turn my attention towards some thing that I was very ill-equipped for, but that was also far bigger than myself: raising a male child as a single mother. Yet, because of my own brokenness, my son's conception was a result of me becoming entangled with a man who was even more self-centered and damaged than my father. Ultimately, my son would pay the price for this accumulated fragility. Though I sought to make my only child my top priority, the truth is, he only ever got to know the version of me who was in a perpetual state of survival…because I had to be. Dysfunctional, generational patterns imprinted within my complex network of nerves were repeating themselves. It wasn't until after my son left home for the military that I became aware that I had been living as a survivor. A mind focused solely on survival cannot thrive. I had to first realize that the safety that I yearned for was mine to create and that I was finally in a place where I could begin to unpack the baggage I had been dragging around my entire life. Through my study of the Bible, and with the help of trusted counselors, the hidden caste system within the social circles that I felt confined to would slowly reveal itself. My criteria have changed for what I will and will not embrace as truth. The feeling of aloneness has transformed into a soothing solitude worthy of my pursuit. And little by little, my Heavenly Father is helping me to re-imagine my sense of identity. And as He would have it, I was to receive a new name to match the season of enlightenment that I was experiencing after years and years of isolation and torment.

My beloved Chinasa, I Am the God Who hears and ANSWERS your prayers.

I must've been in a state of mild shock upon hearing the powerful definition of my new Nigerian name spoken over me on that day under the open African skies. It took my brain a minute to synchronize with my ears to fully understand what happened. In an instant, my identity had been changed. I wasn't entirely conscious of the transformation that would result from answering the call to be a part of this reclamation experience. Still, I can say that my life has never been the same since then.

No longer will I resign myself to accepting less than God's best for me. Nor will I expect others to receive a blessing and I nothing. I am *not* alone. I have *never* been un-wanted by my Heavenly Father. My earthly family has operated out of their hurts, habits, and hang-ups, and I have done the same. Still, my Abba Father has always guarded over me jealously. He has never failed to have a beautiful plan for me. As with the caterpillar, my Father has intentionally done His *best work* in the darkness. God hears and ***answers*** my prayers. A new narrative came with my Ibo name, which changed how I see myself. Now, when Chinasa enters a room, she knows what she carries! I no longer approach the Throne of God as an orphan. That spirit has been *rejected*. And when it tries to worm its way back into my consciousness, I counter it because I am an heir with Christ and accepted into the Beloved. Although I'm still evolving, my life has undergone a profound transformation since I was given a fresh identity.

I currently hold the belief that every person should reserve the right to select their own name at some stage in life. We are not given a choice at birth, but at some point, everyone should decide what name they identify with. Had I never traveled to Nigeria and participated in the ceremony, I would like to think that I would have eventually reached a point in my life when I would have boldly and intentionally adopted a sense of self that aligns with how I have come to understand that God sees me. Participating in such a sacred ritual accelerated my healing and transformation. Nevertheless, there is no need to travel anywhere to directly align with God's perception of me. Through my relationship with God the Father, the Son, and the Holy Spirit, I can come into harmony with the titles that agree with His Truth.

Are YOU ready to uncouple yourself from the lies that come with generational curses and embrace a supernatural Love that will revolutionize your entire life? If so, then I dare you to ask God to reveal to you how *HE* sees you and what He says about you! The beautifully written chapters that follow were crafted with love, passion, and determination. Each Co-Author allowed God to take her on a journey back through the hallways of time and into some painful places and spaces. Each woman accepted God's invitation to draw closer to Him and incline her ear to His heart. And there, above and beyond the noise of adversity, she heard the melody of His song being sung over her (Zephaniah 3:17). None of our lives will ever be the same. Surely, within the eleven stories of this unique cohort of transformational writers, you will be able to see yourself. And maybe, *just maybe*, you will feel compelled to ask the Lover of your soul for a new sense of identification.

My challenge to you is to find a quiet place and take your time to prayerfully read through the chronicle of each woman. Request assistance from the Father as you mine for the pearls embedded within each biographer's difficult *her*story. Be sure to take notes so you can capture them and then ***do something*** with them that will alter your life. We know that we shall all receive new names when we get to Heaven (Rev. 2:17). The Lord desires to grant you a fresh identity to replace the one shattered by thc sin and shame inherent in and around all of us. *Ask Him for it, beloved!* Unlike our earthly parents, who fall short, our Heavenly Father will always answer when we call. He will never shut you out! He will always stick closer to you than a brother. He is NOT like man that He should lie. He will not reject you but will call you His chosen one…and you will never be the same..

REFLECTIONS

MOM

SHANNON WALKER

With every desperate breath, I slowly drew in his smell, imprinting it to memory, touching his warm skin, mapping out the lines in his face, and driving what my senses were experiencing into the depths of my soul. Profoundly aware that his last breaths would also be my last precious memories of us together, continuously telling myself I would never forget.

That was the day time stood still when my world changed forever. It was the day my father died. God blessed me with the precious gift of being there to hold my father's hand. I was able to whisper, "I love you," in the still and quiet moment as his spirit left his body to be reunited with Jesus. My father's gain was my loss, and my loss was just beginning.

My father was the most influential human being that I've ever known on this earth. We were as close as any father and daughter could be. I spoke with him every day. My life's mission was to make him proud. I wondered what he thought about my life's choices, direction, and struggles. Seventeen years after his death, I still wonder if he would be as proud as I would want him to be.

My father often told me, "You'll never know how much I love you until you have your first child." His words were only words to me until the afternoon of April 12, 1995, when my son Jarod Spencer Kendall was born. Nine hours later, in the early hours of April 13th,

Jacob Tyler Kendall was born and put an exclamation point on the revelation that my world would never be the same. I was a mom. Life was not about me anymore. In an instant, I saw everything differently. The world became a more dangerous place, full of uncertainty. I felt inadequate about where I was, my support system, and my ability to lead, provide, and protect. In the blink of an eye, I knew that there was nothing that I wouldn't do for my boys. Two precious souls became my number one priority for the rest of my life. Two human beings I knew that, with out hesitation, I would die for. Yet, I didn't know that "Mom" would ALSO be the name I would *live* for.

At the time, I was not aware of what was happening. I did not know that the name, Mom, and all it represented, would give me the strength, courage, and endurance to face the unknown. To press on, to be my best, and to provide the most for my boys. What I've learned through the years is there has been a focus that caused me to persevere through obstacles. My life was not my own. It never has been. But on this earth, the name Mom became my badge of honor. It would guide every decision I would ever make.

I wanted to give my boys the stable family unit I had the blessing of growing up in. Instead, I divorced their father when they were eleven after a 15-year marriage. Our union was full of anger, fear, conflict, and uncertainty. Out of respect for my boys, I will not elaborate any further.

During that time, I discovered that life consists of what we focus on. I had to learn not to dwell on my mistakes, and that God's grace is sufficient. My attention was on my relationship with God, raising and protecting my boys and building my dog training business so I could be a stay-at-home mom and provide the life I wanted them to have.

It was my heart's desire to give my boys what my mom gave my brothers and me growing up. First and foremost, my mom was a praying mom. She helped raise us with a loving demeanor. She was nurturing, positive, and supportive, celebrating every moment and never missing an opportunity to make us feel special. Our home was always warm, with breakfast and dinner on the table daily. We sat and ate as a family; we were a family. She was a stellar example of grace and kindness. She still is. My boys' home was very different. Due to the need to build my business, instead of home cooked meals and sitting at the table together every night, our time was spent working together and taking care of dogs. Some of my most precious memories are of us walking dogs together, hand in hand, on our four-acre property. They'd share their young-minded thoughts and ask questions. There we were, a Mom and her small boys, talking about anything and everything. They helped me in all aspects of taking care of the dogs. Just the three of us. Those are still some of my most treasured memories.

At 18, the boys changed their last names from Kendall to Walker, my maiden name. Watching them, as young men, stand before the judge was surreal. The power of a name, a last name, the name my father carried, MY name. It was a proud moment for me.

In 2011, I started a nonprofit, Northwest Battle Buddies. Jarod and Jacob worked alongside me like always. In addition to working the family dog training and boarding business, Man's Best Friend, we were now training service dogs for Veterans. This would soon be interrupted by their commitment to serve their country. Jacob enlisted in the United States Army, and Jarod enlisted in the United States Marine Corps. I could not have been prouder.

If I was not a praying mom before, I was for sure a praying mom now. Having my boys deployed on the other side of the world was gut-wrenching. Don't get me wrong: they had my full support. The men and women who serve our country have my greatest respect. My father served in the United States Air Force during the Korean War and taught me to believe in: God, Family, and Country, and "When you are in the presence of a Veteran, you are in the presence of a hero," even though my father never considered himself one. This was the sole reason I founded my nonprofit. However, the passion and belief my father instilled in me did not help this mother's heart as I watched my boys leave on that bus. Emotions of loneliness, uncertainty, and fear quickly joined the moments of pride. I will never forget the first step into our now-empty home. It was just me and my dogs; I was alone for the first time in 21 years.

Jarod served one enlistment, and Jacob served two. This represented years of separation for holidays, birthdays, life tragedies, and triumphs, all shared, celebrated, and endured across the miles. As hard as it was to be apart, the goodbyes were the worst. Jacob especially because his service was the longest. When he was on leave, talking about when he had to return was a forbidden discussion. We wanted to embrace the time together and not even think of being separated again. Packing would always be left until the middle of the night, just hours before his flight left, taking him far away back to his duty station. I'd stay up with him, not wasting a single minute together. I could not allow sleep to steal even one precious moment. Often, time was spent with me sitting on the floor, us talking about nothing, just being together, fully aware that it would be many months before we could hug, talk, and share life up close again. My sons were amazing young men when they enlisted and were mature leaders of men when they got out. I am proud of the men they have chosen to become.

Unlike many parents, my boys finished their enlistments and came home. My heart weeps for the mothers who do not share my joyous experience. May God bring them peace and wholeness daily. Our country will forever be indebted for their sacrifice.

Through the years, hearing them say *Mom* for the first time was just the beginning of life's most wonderful moments. It mattered not whether they yelled out of excitement with something to share or when they were angry at one an other, or when they were sick, hurt, or scared in the night. My heart would leap when they said, "Mom, I love you," randomly throughout the day. My boys are 28 now, and that hasn't changed for me. They might say, "Mom, you want to come to dinner, or Mom, can I talk to you about something I'm thinking about?" We never part ways or end a conversation without saying "I love you." *Ever.*

When I think about my father and how we said, "I love you" to each other teasingly, discussing who loved each other more, he would always win. When reflecting on his words, "You will never know how much I love you until you have your own child," I realize there was no way for me to know the life-changing call to action the title of *Mom* would become.

It's amazing how the most significant and wonderful memories in life can sometimes share the same space as devastating ones. Moments that life-altering decisions are birthed from. Jarod weighed 6 lbs. 5 oz, and Jacob weighed 8 lbs. 11 oz. Jarod was born naturally, and Jacob by cesarean. With the revelation of newfound overwhelming love, purpose, and gratitude to God, I was happier than I had ever been in my life. My then-husband and I took them home two days after their birth. My joy was immediately sucked out of the room by their father's intense anger because the babies were crying. I couldn't get them to stop, and with all of his frustrated outbursts, I pleaded with him to go to bed. "I will take care of it. Please just go." I was anemic, had a hematoma the size of a cantaloupe in my abdomen, was exhausted, and felt totally alone. I vowed at that moment I would never have another child with him.

Life decisions can be made in a heartbeat, and we don't even realize we've just made them. We do the same with adopting names. You may not think you have one, but you do. A name that drives our decisions based on our self-worth. It might've been a sweet nickname given by your grandfather, or what a bully or abuser called you, or even the labels that life has handed you, mother, daughter, son. Consciously or subconsciously we have owned and acted on the names we have claimed in our minds. This name could be a driving force for you to be your best self or the name that devalues your worth and self-image. The greatest conversation we will ever have is the conversation we have with ourselves, and the greatest battlefield is the one in our mind.

Before the age of 28, I was a daughter and a sister to two brothers. The first thing that comes to my mind is that I was *no one*. If I dared to go deeper I must admit I also carried other names. Names like unwanted, lonely, not feminine, rejected, not good enough, and ugly. I spent my days trying to fill the holes in my broken soul with achievement. Preparing my life to need no one or anything, and desperately trying to fill the void that could only be filled with the revelation that I was God's daughter, beautiful and valued by Him. The name Mom has given me strength beyond myself. Many years have contained painful gut-wrenching chapters. That name fueled my purpose, where failure was not an option.

As a child growing up, my parents never allowed us to speak negative, accusing, damaging words to each other. The contrast of my reality as an adult was head spinning. I think, more than not, the negative names that people have called us are unfortunately, more impactful than the positive ones. Names are used in a way to injure our souls. We get called a name and are hurt or offended. And an offense never stays just an offense. It mutates into a personality trait. It's like a cold that can become pneumonia. Emotional injury is inevitable. We cannot avoid it. I have carried unwanted names through the decades of my life. Names I choose not to speak of that were spoken to me by some of the most important people in my life. Names whispered to me in the night launched like a missile straight into my heart. The worst names for any woman to hear. Names I still hear and battle even today.

As I write, tears flow at the thought of what God chooses to call ME; I have been called many names that I did not write about. Names that made me cry, that brought shame and led to sleepless nights for weeks, even months. Names that caused my eyes to drop to the floor, ones I wouldn't want anyone to hear. Names that pierced my soul. Names that bring tears to my eyes along with painful, life-altering memories. I chose to write about what has driven me for the good in my life. No one is exempt from the evil in this world; therefore, I choose to declare all of the names God has for me *and* the name Mom. The greatest compliment, the greatest responsibility, the greatest privilege, the greatest assignment given to me by God. God trusted me and gave me the name that has been my true North.

What is the name that you have chosen to adopt in your life? There will always be a name that is significant, that determines your course, your path, your belief, and your determination. I encourage you to adopt the name your Heavenly Father calls you.

God calls you, the righteousness of God in Christ Jesus, saved, sanctified, the light of the world, the salt of the earth, a city set on a hill, redeemed, loved, chosen, God's own, a chosen generation, overcomer, a royal priesthood, kings and priests, a holy nation, a peculiar person, joint heirs with Christ, and God's child.

What do you say about yourself? Does your name compel you to come up higher? Does it inspire you to be more than you are, or does it allow you to stay in the deep? We all have one. Choose your name and choose wisely.

I would also say to you to declare that you are who God says you are. You are everything God has made you to be and nothing less. Confess and agree because, *again*, God says you are the righteousness of God in Christ Jesus, and you are saved and sanctified by the blood of Jesus. You are not rejected or neglected. Instead, you are loved, chosen, and worthy, and *You are God's own.*

REFLECTIONS

I AM CHOSEN: FROM REJECTED TO APPOINTED

Dr. Judine Berlus

But you, Israel, my servant Jacob, whom I have **chosen,** you descendants of Abraham my friend,[9] I took you from the ends of the earth, from its farthest corners I called you. I said, 'You are my servant'; I have **chosen** you and have not rejected you.[10] So do not fear, for I am with you; do not be dismayed, for I am your God. I will strengthen you and help you; I will uphold you with my righteous right hand." - **Isaiah 41:8-10 (NIV)**

Imagine hearing these words from the divine, Supreme Creator of the heavens and earth, reminding His people, Israel: they are HIS chosen ones. He chose Israel despite their idolatry, their rebellion, and their complaining. He chose them in spite of them *not* choosing HIM.

As I hovered over the verses in Isaiah 41:8-10, I struggled to comprehend why the omniscient, omnipotent, and omnipresent God would choose those who had not *chosen* Him. My simple carnal mind could not transcend into the spiritual dimensions in which God had chosen a nation that, time after time, failed to reciprocate *the choosing*. As I continued to ruminate over this scripture, the Holy Spirit revealed to me that God was intentional with the names He spoke to Israel and the order in which He spoke them. He first called them Israel (who they are in the present and being transformed into), meaning "*one who struggles with God,"* to remind them of who they are to Him and their divine purpose. He then called them Jacob (who they used to be and who they have transformed *from*), meaning "*the supplanter,*" to remind them that He had seen all that they had done, and yet still He *chose* them. The one who spoke the universe into existence, Elohim, understood the power of a name. He understood that the transforming power of a name was integral to the unearthing and fulfillment of one's purpose. This is seen multiple times in Scripture; we see God changing the names of Abram to Abraham, Sarai to Sarah, Jacob to Israel, and Simon to Peter. God in His omniscience is reminding us that in changing their name, He is declaring that they would inevitably be transformed into all He has for them and equipping them for the purpose for which He has called them. God was teaching His people, teaching *me* about the prophetic and transforming power of a name.

To seek clarity and understanding, I decided to research the root word used for chosen in Isaiah 41.8. According to Strongs, the Hebrew word used in the above verse is "*Bachar,*" meaning "to choose, to elect, and to appoint." But how could El Roi, the One who sees, elect and appoint people who exemplified rebellion? I could not comprehend why God had chosen Israel time after time because, in my heart, I was struggling to accept that God could ever choose me. In the book, *The Knowledge of the Holy*, A.W Tozer wrote, "What comes into our minds when we think about God is the most important thing about us." For decades, all that came to my mind when I thought about God, the Father, was *rejection*. I had been birthed into the dark oblivion and the self consuming pit of rejection, gifted to me from my earthly father, and this rejection became the distorted lens through which I would see the Heavenly Father. I had wrestled with God choosing Israel because I never personally experienced the unconditional, unfailing, and unrelenting love from my earthly father. I had not been given the privilege to be Daddy's little girl, so my perception of my Heavenly God was that of judgment and not of love. To rationalize my thoughts and beliefs, I had created an image of God that was incapable of loving me, and this belief fueled my outright refusal and dismissal of the fact that I could ever be chosen by HIM or anyone. Why would God choose me when my earthly father hadn't? How and why would God love me? In my mind, I was the poster child for all things mundane. I was birthed to a single mother, an average student, who had submerged myself in all things of this world to satiate the void that had been etched in my soul. There was something about being rejected by my earthly father that had broken my heart and shattered my spirit. Rejection contorted and commanded my thoughts and relentless accusations to believe that it was because of *me* that my father had not been present: maybe I was not beautiful enough, not refined enough, didn't speak well enough? If my physical father didn't think I was good enough, why would the preeminent God, Yahweh, the great I Am, the King of kings want me? Why would He have interest in this broken and rejected vessel? However, God, who Himself is Love, reached out His purifying and transforming hand to pull me out of the infinitely dark place that had been my permanent dwelling place for so long. In the book *Uninvited*, the author, Lysa Terkeurst, writes "*You will feast on what you focus on.*" For so long, I had focused on the fact that my father had rejected and abandoned me. I replayed the copious number of times he would stop at my neighbor's house that was two doors down and would never come to see me. I remember the missed birthdays, the missed graduations, the missed school events. To pacify the deep anguish in my heart, I would imagine that my father had *chosen* me, hearing his soft voice telling me how much he genuinely loved me. Lysa was indeed right;

I had feasted on rejection for so long that I had given it the power to define who I was. Rejection had significantly skewed my perception of not only the way God saw me but also the way others saw me. I felt unworthy of every relationship and never felt I deserved anything good. I was insecure and became obsessed with pleasing others, fearing they too would reject or abandon me.

However, a series of key events disrupted the false equilibrium of rejection and began to catalyze the transformational shift in my mindset. I was quite fortunate to have been raised in a family of Christians who routinely attended church every Sunday morning. I would say I knew *of* God; however, *I did not know* God. I had religion and not a relationship because I had not encountered God's overwhelming and transforming love. I had heard the same message being taught time after time, with the pastor's attempt to scare believers into outward sanctification by emphasizing the consequences of sin, unknowingly elevating sin over God's love. In other words, the message was familiar and aligned with my distorted beliefs of rejection; Sunday after Sunday, the pastor unknowingly elevated my unworthiness over God's love and, in so doing, validated my belief that God had rejected me. I believe I heard from God for the first time at ten years old. It was not an audible voice, but more like a calm whisper in my spirit that manifested as an irresistible desire to tell my aunt that I no longer wanted to attend church with her, instead, I would attend church with my grandmother. As you can imagine, for a petite, insecure, and timid girl, that seemed like an astronomical task, and I was terrified. However, the burning desire intensified and fueled my courage to speak with my aunt. I remember the day clearly; she was sitting on the verandah in her favorite white chair on the green car porch, about mid-afternoon, and she was doing her favorite puzzles with her feet crossed at the bottom the way they always were. I had lived with my aunt since I was three months old since she had other children and my mom had to work (this was the norm in our culture). I realize how fortunate I have been to have the love of two amazing women (my aunt and mom). My aunt exemplified the love of God; she emanated kindness and patience. She was intentional about speaking life into me. After sheepishly sharing with her that I would like to go to church with my grandma, I remember her simply lifting her head from the puzzle she was working on and asking why. I told her I didn't feel like I belonged at that church. My aunt's response stunned me. She looked keenly into my eyes as if examining the depths of my soul, and with calmness, said, "Okay, no problem." No more questions, no rebuke, no harsh tones. I felt seen, valued, appreciated, and loved. My feelings were acknowledged.

At the age of 18, I moved to the United States to a little town called Macon, Georgia. At that time, my spiritual walk with God was, at best, unstable. I was mad at God. I was alone in a new place, with no family, and I felt abandoned. I was "mad" at God because He never healed my aunt, who died when I was 15. My aunt had been my key cheerleader, and my voice of reason, and she was not around when I needed her most. It was in Macon that I experienced my first intense spiritual attack. It was a Thursday evening, and I was scheduled to work in the gym that day; however, I wasn't feeling well, and I felt so lethargic that I decided to lie down. And that's when it happened. I couldn't move or breathe, but I could finally break free by screaming the name of Jesus. I sat there in a state of shock. That Sunday, I went to church and went to the altar for prayer. As the pastor prayed, he pointed a finger in my face, and I'll never forget His words, he said, "The devil is trying to kill you," I couldn't even respond. I recommitted my life to God and was baptized on December 10, 2002. This time, my walk with God was different. I discovered the power of the Holy Spirit, which allowed me to be in a *relationship* with Christ. For the first time, I experienced and encountered the immense, over whelming, and unconditional power of God's love. I had always known *of* God's love. However, the Holy Spirit opened my spiritual eyes to the magnitude of Christ's love for *me*. Romans 5:8 KJV states, "While we were yet sinners, Christ died for us." In other words, He'd seen me at my very worst, when I was happy and reckless in my rebellion, and He still chose *me*. God gave His only Son to die for you and me. The realization that He had chosen me caused me to cry out from the depths of my soul. I poured out all I had before Him, and I repented for trying so hard to earn His love that He had so freely given. I cried because, for the first time, I could cry out "Abba" and believe I had a Father who loved and saw me for me and still chose me. The encounter with HIS love awakened a boldness and began my lengthy transformation process. The scars of rejection were slowly fading under His love's overwhelming power. I began to embrace His purpose for me and as a profession of faith, I applied to pharmacy school.

In 2004, I was *accepted* into the Lloyd L. Gregory School of Pharmacy. They chose me. I was gradually acclimating to being *chosen* and this feeling anchored me throughout the tedious and challenging years of pharmacy school. In 2008, I graduated magna cum laude with my Doctor of Pharmacy degree. My Abba was slowly elevating me out of the pit of rejection.

In 2009, I had my first ovarian cystectomy and was diagnosed with endometriosis. My physician told me that I might not be able to conceive and that I needed to act urgently if I intended to have children. These words ripped into my core because I always wanted to be a mother. Two years later, I began to experience the same excruciating pain and was informed by my physician once more that I had ovarian cysts on the same ovary. I would need to have the same procedure to have the cysts and my ovary removed. I was beyond devastated and fervently sought God through prayer and fasting for direction on how to proceed. God saw me in my brokenness and whispered gently in my spirit. The morning of the surgery, when the physician came to check in, I told him I would prefer not to have my ovary removed, and to my surprise, he said he was coming to tell me the same thing! This reinforced that I was indeed hearing from God. After the ovarian cystectomy, while waiting in recovery, I saw my physician slowly approaching the room with a puzzled look. I'll never forget his words. He said, "Well, it seems your body likes to throw cysts because there was a cyst, but your endometriosis is gone." *Gone*?? "Yes, gone." My Abba Father had *chosen* to HEAL *me*. Six years later, I miraculously gave birth to a beautiful, healthy baby boy after trying for almost seven years to conceive.

Not only was God continuously elevating me from the pit of rejection, He was gifting me with uncommon favor, and placing me on the path of divine blessings. In May 2012, I was accepted into the Johns Hopkins School of Public Health. I was overwhelmed with gratitude that once again I had been *chosen*. In May of 2013, I graduated with honors with a Master of Public Health.

In December 2017, there was a realignment in the company where I was working, and many of my colleagues were terrified that we could lose our jobs, especially right before Christmas. The entire team was panic-stricken, with the glooming cloud of uncertainty that engulfed us. We were all assigned appointments to be informed of whether our positions would be eliminated or be one of the fortunate few to be chosen for promotion. My appointment was at 3 p.m. and I was terrified because I was one of the newest supervisors on the team and had been in the role for less than six months. At 3 p.m., the HR director summoned me to the office. As I entered the tense room, I was greeted by the emotionless face of my Regional Director sitting squarely at his desk, his posture cold and stoic. As I sat down, I was promptly handed a folder. I hesitantly opened it, and as I read through, relief flooded through my body. They had decided to promote me to the new position. Once again, God allowed me the privilege of being *chosen* and granted me divine unmerited favor. He reminded me that He was EL Roi, the God who sees me.

As my chosen journey continued, on December 4, 2021, I had the distinct honor of being ordained as a Pastor and Prophetess in Adonai Healing Temple Ministries International church, founded in Jamaica. Before being ordained, the traces of rejection resurfaced, leading me to my closet to "confirm" with God that He wanted me. I remember His soft but sharp rebuke of me doubting Him and His purpose for my life. As I knelt on my knees, with tears streaming down my cheeks, I repented before God, and once more simply received His choosing.

As I reflect on the trajectory of my life, I am beyond grateful for God's unfailing love. I included my accomplishments not out of arrogance but as a testimony of how He relentlessly pursued and continues to pursue me. The revelation of God Himself as love is needed to combat the daily battle with rejection. He has called me CHOSEN, and I'm being transformed into His image daily and walking in the purpose He has called me to. In the same way, He chose Israel, He chose me.

To all those engulfed in the deep dark trenches of rejection, I kindly ask that you focus on this truth: God loves YOU. He loves you so much, He gave His only son for YOU. He loves you so much, He inscribed YOUR name in the palm of His hands. Before He formed you in the womb, He set YOU apart for Himself. YOU are chosen for HIS purpose. Be intentional about basking in His presence to behold His glory and experience His love. In other words, as the author Jackie Hill Perry states in the book *Holier than Thou*, "Lasting transformation is a spiritual consequence of beholding the Glory of the Lord."

REFLECTIONS

DAUGHTER

DIANNE REID

The sun had just woken up to start its shift. It was fighting with the clouds for its turn to shine. It was Sunday and my parents were in their normal routine of getting the family ready for church. Behind closed doors, unbelief took refuge in my parents apartment and demanded stillness. On this day, as they turned on the news to check the weather, they found all the channels reporting the same message. "Earlier this morning in Paris, France, Princess Diana was killed in a fatal car crash trying to escape paparazzi." On this side of the world in the Bronx, NY, my mom was crying tears that could re-fill the body of water that separated the two continents. My two older sisters, six and eleven at the time, were trying to fully grasp what was happening and why our mother was crying so much. As a Jamaican, my mom held an affinity towards the British royals, specifically Princess Diana, because she was the most relatable and lovable of them all. This day was August 31, 1997. I was to be born four months later. My mom sometimes tries to deny it but my dad will absolutely confirm that I was named after Princess Diana. My mom decided that Dianne was the perfect name for me. She hated "A's" at the end of names and believed adding two "Ns" would make the name more unique. I was named after a princess whose life demanded her to be perfect and above reproach, and who died running from attention. Who knew that that would set the tone for a daughter trying to find her place in the world?

The word "daughter" symbolizes a form of acceptance and a love that does not need to be earned. No matter what I do, I can't change the fact that I am a daughter. As a child of my Jamaican parents, there was little to no room for error. "Back in Jamaica, I only had two shoes, one for church and one for school. We worked hard for the opportunities you have today. Don't waste it. Don't embarrass us in the street. Do better than everyone else." Those were the common phrases that were embedded in my brain as a child. Then reinforced through interactions with my parents.

In fourth grade, I excitedly came home with a 97 on a test. I was prepared for my mom to grab me in her arms and tell me how proud she was of my academic achievement. However, her first response was a question, "What did everyone else get?" My mistake was saying a grade higher than 97 that someone else received. Her retort was, "Why didn't you score higher than them?" My enthusiasm completely subsided and turned into disappointment in myself and feelings of rejection. I wanted my mother to share in my happiness but instead, she stole it away from me. I felt like being me was not enough to be affirmed and praised. My value was based on the people around me and how I measured up. As a result, I learned to compare my achievements and actions to others at an early age. I know this was not my mother's intent. She was probably trying to hold me to a standard. However, with that level of comparison, there was no way that thought process would not seep into other areas of my life. If my mother is supposed to be one who loves me without borders, and she didn't accept me, then being me was not good enough.

The summer of the following year my family was hosting a summer barbecue at our home. The smell of scotch bonnet, allspice, and black pepper danced in the air with the wind playing the melody. "Bam Bam" by Reggae artist Sister Nancy was the theme song playing as Dominos smacked on the table. Cousins passionately trash-talked and discussed the latest music artists. I began to share my perspective in conversation. Mid-point, but at the end of my sentence, my oldest sister said mockingly, "You talk like a Valley girl." I'm ten years old at this point. I have no reference for the valley or how people from there speak. She clarified while laughing, "Like a white girl." Ridicule and rejection overwhelmed me, and I yelled, "I'm not a Valley girl!" She assuredly said, "No, but you talk like one." She said what she said because I was speaking proper English. It was an assault on my identity as the daughter of Jamaicans. Here was another person who I thought was to love me--no matter what--asking me to change something else about me. I believed I wasn't fully accepted by my parents and at the same time feeling mocked and disregarded by my siblings. Surely there was a place where I could exist as my authentic self and not feel the need to hide or morph into something else to be affirmed.

At the backdrop of my entire life was the church. I was essentially born and raised there, too. "Come as you are", was a phrase introduced to me early. Once I came into a knowing of what that phrase meant, I was ready to be in an environment where I could just be me. By around twelve years old that was not true. I witnessed the older people in the church gossiping about children's bad behavior and how that was an indictment on their parents. My parents and older sister were well-known people in the church. My dad was known as the deacon and Bible teacher who could pray heaven down. My mom was a deaconess and volunteer. I was often referred to as "Deacon Reid's kid". I was only known by the persona placed on me and not who I was. I also added the pressure of not wanting to let my family look bad. I did not want to embarrass the family. Consequently, I put on a performance. I acted like I knew the Bible and had a strong relationship because that was what others assumed. When in reality, I rarely prayed and read my Bible even less.

If perfection was what God's people expected, and being the best was what my parents required, how much more perfection did a perfect God want from me? I never spoke to God because I never felt like He wanted to talk to me. It seemed like no one in my universe desired to be with the real me. Who was I to think the God of the whole universe would be waiting to hear from me? Nowhere felt like a safe place.

It appeared that I was not authentically loved anywhere, especially not in the places people professed to openly. This caused an emptiness that opened the door for addiction to form. My feelings of rejection and loneliness led me to find solace in pornography and masturbation. My introduction to sexual content happened at the age of 11 or 12. This was the same time I internalized feelings of not being seen in arenas where unconditional love was to reside. The perfect storm of a present problem and seemingly correct solution. Masturbation provided an immediate escape from present pain and momentary satisfaction. It wasn't just satisfaction. It is how my child mind registered love. I watched a lot of romance movies as a younger child and it was quite apparent that people who romantically love each other had sexual relations. From the ages of eleven to twenty-three, I fabricated the desire for approval I was searching for through controlled, instant satisfaction. It was reliable. It didn't disappoint me. And yet, I still felt unseen and unknown because once the moment of high passed, I was still left with me. When the truth was, I wanted people to choose the real me. However, if someone were to really know me, I first had to stop acting in the role of someone working to be loved.

What actors don't tell you is how exhausting it is to be an actor. Some actors say they have to take a month or two off after a project because they have to get reacquainted with themselves. A return to home base. However, they voluntarily sign up for that profession. Many actors understand the recovery techniques needed to get back to their true selves. But what happens when you don't know you're acting? There is no return back to self. There is no home base. I had to keep track of what character I needed to be depending on what group I was around. By the time I was 23, I was tired of my one-man Broadway show. I was exhausted by my characters. I was depleted, not truly known, and alone. Then in 2020, COVID-19 devastatingly hit America and forced the entire world to stop their daily routines and be in solitary places. There I was in my one-bedroom apartment in Pittsburgh, Pennsylvania miles away from family and friends I grew up with. This was partially beneficial because I didn't have to perform in the world anymore because the world was just shut down. Unfortunately, the outward solitude matched my inward isolation. I was forced to confront my truest reality. I lived my life as a vagabond in search of a place to call home. Where is home? Where safety, recognition, and unconditional love reside. So I leaned on the only person who encompassed all those characteristics. God.

I started to have real conversations with Him. I asked questions like, "Lord, what is my purpose? Why did you create me?" At that time, it was hard to see the purpose of anything, let alone myself. But even in asking questions, I was focused on how I had to show up and perform for God because that was all I knew. But the more I talked to God, the more He showed me Him. The more He showed me Him, the more I saw myself. I am a reflection of God, but not in the church performative way. In the way that He created me in His image. However,

I am not just an image bearer of the Most High. Because I confess with my mouth Jesus Is Lord and believe in my heart that God raised Him from the dead, I am a child of God.

The name that I choose is no longer a daughter of Jamaican immigrants or the daughter of powerful, faith-filled parents but a daughter of the King of kings (God). A different kind of "princess." In this, my life is built on Someone who knows me better than me because He created me. Everything God created He called it good. Therefore, I am good just because I exist, not because of anything I do or how I perform but because I am here.

April 8th, 2023 was the day of my official solidification of my identity in Him by addressing all the ways I performed for adoration. He told me a couple of mindset-shifting words that forced me into a new direction. I did not realize the Lord was directly speaking to me as His daughter. He said, "I love you more than you can comprehend: rest in my love." God is love. God is constant. God is trustworthy. So, God's love is constant and trustworthy. And I can't earn it or perform for it. I can't create it by manufacturing instant pleasure. I also can't lose it. I could finally rest. God loves me so much that He sent His only begotten Son to die for my sins. God also said, "No longer will you compare your anointing to those around you. You are unique. You will never fit in because you were born to stand out." How dare the Lord throw out my measuring stick?!? I could no longer compare my life and impact to anyone else because no one is me. Comparison was killing my identity. It made me focus so much on other people that I never truly focused on what made me unique.

I am still learning to walk in my title as daughter of the King [God]. It is a daily choice. After years of hiding myself, some of those old thoughts of inadequacy try to come back. I have to actively remind myself of who I am in a world that tries to discourage me. But I choose to own my royalty.

I am loved. I am called. I am favored. I am chosen. I am a co-heir with Christ and a daughter of the King [God]. This moniker comes with authority and promises. I am responsible for owning and living as the me God created. One of those responsibilities is that His glory is revealed through my life and uniqueness. The more I downplay or hide, the more I limit the glory of God that is revealed through my life. One of the promises that come from being a child of God is abundant life. Not just financial abundance. A life filled with peace, patience, joy, and love. All the aspects of life I was in constant search of. Not knowing it was in my grasp the entire time.

Fortunately, this isn't unique to me. God wants you to rest in Him, too. He already loves you. Pass your masks, flaws, mess-ups, and ways to manufacture fleeting versions of love. God is all that you are in search of, and He yearns to be with you. The more you are with Him, the more accurately you will view YOU. When you place your attention and focus on the God who never changes, you receive an unbreakable confidence that cannot be given or taken by the world. You begin to realize that your differences were intentional. You were created on purpose for a purpose. He created you because the world needed you.

Who are you? What are you calling yourself? Does it align with what God says about you? Own the name God calls you and see how your life shifts for the better.

You are called. You are loved. You are favored. You are chosen. Choose to accept your identity in Christ today!

Below are some Scriptures that remind me of the unshakable love of God:

"For God so loved the world that he gave his one and only Son, that whoever believes in him shall not perish but have eternal life."
John 3:16

"For I am convinced that neither death nor life, neither angels nor demons, neither the present nor the future, nor any powers, neither height nor depth, nor anything else in all creation, will be able to separate us from the love of God that is in Christ Jesus our Lord."
Romans 8:35-39

"For you created my innermost being; you knit me together in my mother's womb. I praise you because I am fear fully and wonderfully made; your works are wonderful, I know that full well."
Psalm 139:13-16

REFLECTIONS

EMBRACING THE PROMISES OF KIKELOMAN (KEE-KEH-LOHMAN)

Sophia K. Tade

"I am a little pencil in God's hands. He does the thinking. He does the writing. He does everything, and sometimes it is really hard because it is a broken pencil, and He has to sharpen it a little more."

Mother Teresa, The Joy in Loving: A Guide to Daily Living

"Who do you think you are? Who cares about what you have to say? No one cares because **you** are an impostor." These words hammered and scattered my heart for a few hours after being asked to co-author this divine assignment on *The Transformative Power of a Name*. Yes, the impostor syndrome was full-on as I chose to listen to another voice. The voice of the Holy Spirit, this loving voice that spoke "healing, peace, revival, joy, success, and hope" to me when I accepted Christ as my Savior. I remembered whose I was, a beloved child of God. I took a deep breath and surrendered to hope versus fear. It is never a victorious battle as the brain keeps trying to take us back into the darkness, the places that hurt, or the past. It takes an intentional, faith-based decision--moment by moment--to keep looking at the Light. And yes, in Jesus Christ I will continue to put my trust.

Full disclosure here, the courage to believe that the PAST IS TRULY GONE did not come to me easily. Truth be told, I still struggle with the idea sometimes. But each time I catch myself, I purposely stop this negative trend of thought by saying something like "CANCEL, CANCEL", or saying a short prayer. Jeremiah 29:11 is a personal favorite. I also remind myself whose I am and what kind of God I serve. It's a moment-to-moment battle, and I would rather have victories than succumb to the vicious circle of nonstop negative self-talk.

I believe there is something fascinating about names. They have power. Power to uplift or power to break. They impart something meaningful to their bearer. My name is Sophia and I received it right after birth. It was repeated over and over to me, became part of my identity, and carried a host of emotions such as love, rejection, fondness and sadness. Love means wisdom. Sadness arrived when I remembered that I was named after my father's ex-fiancée who never married. A heaviness settles in when I think about the fact that Sophia is the only name I have on my birth certificate. And these emotions are based on the belief I gave to the meaning of my name. Quite powerful. This reminds me of the story of Jabez in 1 Chronicles 10:1 KJV. I learned that his name means "born in sorrow and pain." Imagine being reminded of this every time it was spoken that his mother named him Jabez because of the pain she endured in labor. No wonder Jabez himself came to believe for some time that his life was defined by pain and sorrow.

I am grateful my mother didn't name me after the pain she endured during labor like Jabez's mother did. And I don't know about you, but I think belief is everything. My thoughts and actions are a direct reflection of my belief system. The person I believe myself to be is the person I become. Belief doesn't care about truth or lies. It just takes the shape of thoughts, emotions, and feelings as indicated in Proverbs 23:7 KJV – "for as he thinketh in his heart, so is he".

I realized at my core how accurate this truth was on January 14, 2013, while sitting by my father's side as tears of relief, gratitude, and joy scrolled down my face. I had come to say goodbye to my father before flying back to the U.S. a few days later. We were at his simple but beautiful home in Porto-Novo (Benin, West Africa) where he was recovering from a massive stroke. It was around 3 p.m., and my father had just awakened from his midday nap. After praying for the usual travel mercies, a good husband, children, and my overall success, he said, "Remember that question you asked me last week about your Yoruba name?" Before I could answer, he added, "I couldn't recall it at the time, but was sure my father sent me a name for each one of you on the day of your birth. And he was still alive when you were born." I looked at him in disbelief as I replied: "Yes Papa, I remember." He continued, "Well, yours is **Kikeloman**. I looked in my folder and found my notes…see?" He showed me his notes. "Kikeloman, the cherished one, the one who is nurtured with love and tenderness, the one who is surrounded by the utmost care."

Still in disbelief, I thought to myself: *What? I had a Yoruba name?* My heart skipped a beat, then uncontrollable tears started scrolling down my face. My dad could not comprehend all the emotions his revelation seemed to cause in me. I was next to him and just hugged him tight for a long moment, wetting his blue bouba (long traditional kaftan for men) with my tears. He kept asking, "Sosso (my nickname), everything ok?" When I could finally speak, I said "Yes, thank you, Papa. I always thought something was wrong with me, and that this was why Baba Tade (my grandfather) didn't give me a Yoruba name."

He asked, "This is why you are crying?" He still couldn't grasp the full impact his words had on me, but for me, a dark veil was gradually tearing down as the light of profound relief and love for myself entered my being inch by inch. A moment I will cherish forever. My father, my beloved Papa, passed away less than a year after our conversation.

You see, my father didn't realize what such a small omission on my birth certificate could cause in my thoughts because as a father, I am sure he loved all his children, and me even more. But for me, growing up, this was no small omission. It was another piece of evidence that I did not belong and that I was not lovable. I used to believe at a very young age that I was cursed from birth, that I would never amount to anything positive in life, and that everyone was good and I was not. *How a five-year-old child can be a bad person, I don't know, but that was my perception.* Maybe it was from the fact that in West Africa people easily believe that some are born blessed and others are cursed for life. Or that people who suffer in this present life are paying the price for bad deeds they have done in a prior life. Maybe the fact that I didn't have a Yoruba name like all my siblings. Or even a combination of different wrong ideas that cumulated in my young brain to give me this false identity? Who knows. Bottom line is, I believed I was not worth it and that thought shaped over 30 years of my life.

Looking back, I can see how my little brain could choose to believe that I didn't get a Yoruba name because my grandfather could see who I was going to be in life, and decided it wasn't worth the effort. And here is why. My grandparents emigrated from Nigeria in the early 1900s and settled down in Porto-Novo, the capital of the Benin Republic, where all their children were born. My grandfather, Baba Tade, was a highly regarded spiritual leader, and counselor to King Toffa and the dignitaries of the city of Porto-Novo. He was perceived as a seer and a sought-after natural healer. King Toffa relied on him for political and judiciary matters. Those who knew him often shared with me instances of his integrity and wisdom, how his decisions were always right and just and how politicians sought after him in selecting the best leaders. So, I thought if I didn't receive a name from this wise man, there was probably something wrong with me. Crazy but true in my mind.

In addition, in Yoruba customs *"Sophia"* would be considered my "foreign name", but *"Kikeloman"* would be perceived as the link to our traditions, our roots, my ancestral lineage, my ethnic group and what I stand for in the world. In my young mind and up until January 14, 2013, I thought I didn't receive my traditional name because of something *negative* my grandfather "*saw*" in me.

From that point, my life experience was fed through those lenses. I grew up being honestly surprised when something good would happen to me and mainly expected the worst to always be my portion. I recall in 9th grade, one of my poems was chosen for best poem of the year by IFR (International French Radio). I thought, "Hmm, it's probably because the really good candidates didn't submit their poems this year". Back then, IFR reached about 67 million French speaking auditors and any student could submit a poem. Yet, I second-guessed this award, including any additional one I received for most of my life. At a personal level, I always expected my boyfriends to leave me and they did--one after the other. If I could not see my true value, how did I expect anyone else to see it?

Logically, my life had to reflect that perception. Everything anyone did, or did not do, had to match my self-fulfilling prophecy. In my mind, my parents' rigor towards me was because they obviously didn't love me. My dad was fine with my brothers and sisters bringing an A- home, but never with me. The only grade I would get an accolade for was A+, nothing less. I now know that it was because he saw my potential and was trying his best to push me to see it. But back then, it didn't feel like that. I thought the only way to my parents' hearts was to be perfect with my grades and everything else. And every time I had an A- or B+, it was as if the world was about to fall on me, reminding me that I was not worth it, would never be enough, and was not lovable.

What I came to realize over time is that these statements are usually not true, but they get stamina through my focus on them, or my looking for evidence to feed my beliefs. The backlash of this is that because I felt like no one cared about me or thought I was worth it, I had to prove myself by collecting the most awards and accolades in everything I did. As a result, I became very studious and did my best to please everyone around me, sacrificing my wants to make someone else happy. I figured by bribing everyone, they would have no choice but to like me. I was described as most helpful, kind, and generous. Yet I felt awkward in groups and had few friends. That impostor feeling was always present because I didn't think there was anything worth it about me; my constant thought was that people would leave me as soon as they found out who I truly was. At some point, frustrated and mentally exhausted, I realized that going the extra mile for friends and siblings didn't make them like me more than others who didn't even do half of what I was doing for them.

So, I was back to square one most of the time, hammering this thought in my head: there is something inherently wrong with you, Sosso. Maybe the deities made you this way to punish you for past wrongs; maybe you are just that unlikable person. To add insult, I held on to every single mistake, thinking about them repeatedly, feeling guilty beyond words, and trapped in this cage with no way out. Feeling trapped as unworthy. Trapped as the impostor in the room. Trapped as the one who truly doesn't belong anywhere. And it seemed like I couldn't help but make mistake after mistake, or go silent, because I was afraid my dad would blame me for what happened to me. So, I chose silence when a relative abused me at 14. I chose silence when our family doctor was inappropriate during a physical examination. I felt dirty. I felt those who preyed on me were not after anyone else because everyone else was good and worth it. No wonder I would put myself last, give my seat away, and help friends complete their papers when mine were still incomplete. The future was quite gloomy for me already. *So why bother*, I thought. At times, it felt like I was in a caste system of my own, the caste of the losers, the group of those who do not amount to much in life.

But today, I give God glory and honor for allowing me to walk back to Him. I credit that moment with my father as the pivotal point of my path to self-healing and self-love. During the last part of our conversation, papa shared that the clerk at the courthouse forgot to add Kikeloman to my birth certificate, and my parents didn't make much of it. It was a simple omission. From Sophia, the unlovable one, to Kikeloman, the cherished one. What a gap! All those years I spent building a case as to why I was not worth it; all these blocks were made of sand, and I am the one that gave them rock-like strength.

I choose to continue to walk by faith, to stand on the promises of Kikeloman, this strong, perseverant, generous, nurturing, and loving soul. This soul gave her life to the Lord. This soul believes that through prayer and hard work, she can lift her siblings and community and co-create intergenerational wealth starting with this generation. As Kikeloman, I choose to trust in what the Scripture tells me. All it took was a decision. So, mine is to grow my faith and stop dwelling in the past because it's gone. My loving dad is gone. My beautiful and strong mother is also gone. What happened to me before today is all gone. By continuing to linger in the past, I remain stuck, living a life of fear, anxiety, and sorrow. But trusting in the Lord when He tells me to let go and to let Him take charge is freeing. I believe that God is not a man that He shall lie. I choose to live from the bright future I am co-creating now with God for His glory. I choose to surrender completely to Him and His ways.

My battle is far from finished. But I am confident that God's mercies are made new each morning, giving me a new blank slate to start over and do better. I choose to be like Jabez who prayed and spoke against the testimony of his name. The Scripture tells us God granted his request. Jabez let go of the shame his name covered him in. God enlarged his territory and made him the most successful of all his siblings. When you pray, come to God vulnerable and ready for Him to turn your weakness into His glory. God's plans for those who love Him are to prosper and give them strength for today and bright hope for tomorrow. Therefore, my only option is to continue to surrender to His will and accept, at my core, as a devoted servant of the Lord, that I too have a place at the table.

And I pray that despite your past and what people told you about who you are, you realize that you, too, are favored. The Lord we serve is merciful! He loves us and set us free at the Cross. We are His arms and legs on this Earth. He wants to use us if we are willing and ready to work for Him and with Him. This is my truth, and you can make it yours too! Keep believing this, reminding yourself of it, and trusting Him.

REFLECTIONS

WHAT'S IN A NAME

Brittani Wegner

What's in a name? When you really think about it – we have no say in it and we can't choose it. It is simply given to us. When we're born, we don't even know what it is. It takes a long time to recognize that it belongs to us and a lot of practice spelling it right. So, why are we given one?

A name is meant to reveal an aspect of a person's identity. If you look in the Bible, God has many names to reveal His character and His nature. And we, being made in the image of God (Genesis 1:27 NIV), have been given many names to reveal our character and nature, as well. So, I knew there was no mistake in the name I was given at birth. The arrangement of alphabets slated as my identity has intent, reason, and purpose - even if I haven't fully walked it out yet.

And, boy, has walking it out been a journey.

My name is Brittani, and I can't recall the first time I recognized it, the first time I said it, or the first time I could spell it, but I do remember the many different names I was given instead of it.

It was my sophomore year of high school, and even though I was almost halfway through, it was a tough year already. I was in the midst of a fight with my two closest girlfriends, and I dreaded going to school. It was January, and the cold on the outside of the school matched the cold I felt on the inside of it. Luckily, our lockers were not very close, and we only had a couple of classes together – but I dreaded those classes most of all because they were not shy about vocalizing their distaste for me, and there was no escaping them.

So, there I went into class and to my seat. And then it began. They started calling me horrible names, loudly and under their breath, in the middle of class. "Slut!" "Whore!" And although my girlfriends and I had gotten into many fights over the years, this one seemed the worst of all. So, I sat there as those words were spoken over me – over and over again – and I said nothing. Why didn't I say anything? Why didn't I defend myself?

Sad to admit, this was not the first time I was called something other than Brittani. In my younger years, my brother would hurl backhanded compliments at me. He started with basic slandering words like stupid and dumb.

When those didn't get enough of a reaction out of me, he switched to words like fat and ugly. And boy did that work. The sheer hatred and disgust in which he used those labels led me to tears every single time. They hurt me deeply.

Now, my parents were divorced, and my mom was so sick of us fighting (and being unable to stop it) that she basically gave up and let us fight it out. And even though my brother was 13 months younger than me, I always ended up on the losing end of the battle. But worst of all, I started to believe the names he gave me were actually mine – that this was my identity.

Now, I didn't believe my brother's words about me right away. I mean, let's be real, "Girls rule, and boys drool." But when my mother gave up on stopping it, that's when my little kid brain tried to make sense of why. I needed a protector, and there was none to be found.

So, in my mind, I thought, *It must be true. That must be why no one loved me enough to stand up for me. That's why no one came to my defense to protect me.* So, I started to believe that these labels truly described who I was, my character, and my nature, and then my brain continually looked for evidence to build a case as to why this must be true.

Then later, when a similar thing happened with my girlfriends in high school, I already had a case built for it. My beliefs were already formed that something was wrong with me and that my identity was flawed. And because I was so used to not being protected or defended, I didn't even know how to defend myself against them. So, while their words hurt, what hurt even more was my belief that everything said about me was true and that there was nothing I could do about it. With my case now built, it was time for me to gather up all my evidence to bring this case to trial. What's funny about a case you've built up against yourself – is that the evidence all comes from yourself. What's sad about this process is that none of this was logically done – my belief, my conclusions, my evidence – they were all formed subconsciously in my little kid brain, a brain that wasn't even fully developed yet. John 8:44 NIV says this about the devil, "When he lies, he speaks his native language, for he is a liar and the father of lies." I didn't realize it at the time, but I was partnering with the adversary by agreeing with the names spoken over me. And then this became the lens that I saw everything through.

While I didn't choose the name given to me at birth, I did subconsciously choose to allow the slander spoken over me to be what defined me. I thought if I could just fix my character and nature of fat and ugly, then I would be worthy to receive a new name of *loved*. This led me down a negative path where I was willing to do anything to get it. So, when attention was given to me by boys in high school, I enjoyed it, and I sought it out. It was almost a way to prove to myself that I could still be loved by a male in my fat and ugly. So, while my actions served as a coping mechanism, it didn't heal the root of my problem. Because, at my core, I still believed that my identity was flawed.

Later, when my high school boyfriend broke up with me, that was the final straw. In my mind, that proved that a male couldn't love me, and I needed to take drastic measures. I then developed an eating disorder to fix my problem. Because fat was my problem, skinny would be my solution. But, because I let the world and its people define me, it didn't take long to realize that that measuring stick is constantly changing. No matter what I did, I couldn't achieve the perfection I sought to be worthy of love, and I kept coming up short. In my mind, I had solidified the case against myself so well that it took something much more than physical changes for me to see things correctly. I not only needed a shift, I needed a mindset shift.

I had to reopen the case I held against myself and look back through all my so-called evidence. In doing so, I discovered three ways I partnered with the enemy when building my case against myself:

First, I operated in judgment. Matthew 7:1 NIV says, "Judge not or you will be judged." God gave me this instruction because He knew I would not be able to judge rightly. I am not an all-powerful and all-knowing being, which means my judgment is from a limited perspective, a flawed lens. This is why, instead of judgment, God gave me discernment. But what did I do? I took my incorrect judgment, made an assessment, and then told myself that my identity was flawed, that I didn't measure up, and that I was a problem that needed fixing to be loved.

Second, I operated in shame. When I concluded that there was something wrong with me, shame entered. I know shame was not a part of God's original intent because Genesis 2:25 NIV states, "Adam and his wife were both naked and they felt no shame." After Adam and Eve ate from the Tree of Knowledge of Good and Evil, their eyes were open, and they felt shame (Genesis 3:7 NIV). Likewise, because of my assessment, I became ashamed of myself for the reason I concluded, in my judgment, that I was not lovable.

Third, I operated in blame. I know that blame was not a part of God's original intent because the Bible does not reference blame until after the fall. In Genesis 3:11-12 NIV, God is asking Adam who told him he was naked, and Adam replied, "The woman you put here with me …" Adam blamed Eve for his decision, his agreement, to consume the fruit of the Tree of Knowledge of Good and Evil. Similarly, in my judgment, I blamed myself for not being lovable.

I was punishing that younger version of myself for being the culprit, the reason for my case of not being lovable. And even though there was no actual truth to support my belief, that younger version of myself was held captive and became a prisoner of my judgment. So, what changed? How did that younger version get free from imprisonment? God.

With God's help, I learned the secret weapon to combat this: forgiveness. Did I need to forgive my brother and my friends for the hurtful words they said about me? Absolutely. But, remember, I wasn't captive because of their words, and it wasn't their words that kept me a prisoner awaiting trial. It was my agreeing with them and then my addition of judgment, shame, and blame. So, who did I most need to forgive? Myself. Those younger versions of me that I held captive and held prisoner.

Once I forgave those younger versions of myself, I could accept God's love in a newfound way. The hole in my heart was ready to be filled by the only One who could fill it. A God whose love does not change based on what I do and is not contingent on my appearance. He made me and I am wonderfully made (Psalm 149:13 NIV). I had already been given the name of *loved* by my Creator (Jeremiah 31:3 NIV), and nothing additional was required of me to make it mine. So that was the journey that God called me to.

So, God led me on a path to start my inner healing journey. It began with an online course and that stirred up my hunger for more. And as I began to learn about myself, I became more self-aware. I didn't realize then that my journey to learn more about myself was also a journey to learn more about God. So, because I am made in His image, an awareness of myself gives me an awareness of Him. It also helped me separate which portions of myself were aligned with God and which were not so that I could bring healing into those areas. God showed me what real love is and what it means to let Him define me rather than the world and those in it.

As my inner world began to be reshaped and reformed, it was time for a new identity--something to represent the new me that I was becoming (2 Corinthians 5:17 NIV). God can and will give you a new name, and He will use your original one as the foundation. Just look at Abraham – Abraham's original name was Abram, which means high father. When God was ready to take him on a journey to discover a new aspect of his nature, it was changed from Abram to Abraham (Genesis 17:5 NIV), which means father of many. So not only do these definitions describe Abraham and the destiny God laid out for him, but they also describe the nature of God!

God decides when it is time to reveal this new nature. However, if you do not ask, you do not receive (James 4:2). So, I felt led to ask God what my new name was. When I did, I was amazed at what was revealed. The name I got was Britannia (see Wikipedia). And while I'm still working out the details of the definition, the image speaks for itself. It is an image of a female warrior, wearing a helmet, holding a spear and shield, with a lion at her side. To me, she represents victory, power, and unity.

At the time when this new identity was given to me by God, I was not feeling at all like this image. I was getting stronger in my identity in Him, but I still had a long way to go to release the strongholds that tied me to the fear of man and what others thought of me. But that's the beauty of God's timing. He told me that He was starting my journey of discovering my true self, and who He says I am – the warrior inside that had been covered up. I liken it to Abraham and when he received his name change to be a father of many when he had no children with his wife Sarah who was 100 years old.

When God reveals these things, it may not look as He describes, but just as Romans 4:17 NIV outlines, God "… calls into being things that were not."

Little by little, I started to step into this new identity of Britannia. God showed me how He uniquely made me, giving me victory over the previous words spoken over me. He showed me how much authority I have, giving me power in my voice. He showed me how much He loves and accepts me for who I am, which created unity within me. I can now confidently say that I am walking in the new name God has given me.

So, I encourage you to take a moment to ask God for your new name and the way He reveals it to you. It may take some time, but be expectant for what He has in store. Because, I promise you, it is better than you can ask, think, or imagine. Let that new identity represent you and erase any other negative or slanderous names you were given, either by yourself or others. And then trust God in the process because "... He who began a good work in you will carry it on to completion until the day of Christ Jesus" (Philippians 1:6 NIV). And there is no one better to give you a new name than the One who created you!

REFLECTIONS

REJECTED TO REDEEMED: ONE OF GOD'S CHOSEN

KEM S. KITCHEN

CHOSEN… All I ever wanted was to be accepted by the people I loved and those who supposedly loved me. I wanted to be accepted for who I was, not for who someone wanted me to be. Was I asking for too much?

From the beginning of this collaborative writing process, I knew what stories I had in mind. The problem was I didn't have the transformation I thought was needed to complete my chapter. As a result, I struggled to engage in the process, at least initially. It's difficult to write about the transformative power of a name when I feel as if I haven't been transformed yet. I'm still a caterpillar moving toward the next phase. Nevertheless, my heart's greatest desire is to complete the process of healing and transformation into the big, beautiful butterfly I was chosen to become. Although this might not seem like the point for a dramatic change, I know writing this chapter is a critical step in my healing journey.

My story began long before I knew the intricate details of the day when rejection would slap me in the face and welcome me to the real world. From that point onward, I would never be the same. One of the people who I loved the most was a person who seemed to love me the least. Even before my mother gave birth, my father rejected me. He denied I was his child until he realized we shared birth defects (dimples and six fingers). After seeing me – my brown skin, the pinkness on the inside of my hands and the bottom of my feet, the blueness of my veins – my father nicknamed me Peacock. It was a unique name I would later embrace as a beautiful representation of me and my business. Like the peacock, I was proud, passionate, purposeful, and peculiar. Sadly, this acceptance from him was only temporary. He would reject me again and again, sometimes without me realizing it. This repeated rejection became evident years later as my mother recounted stories of my father bragging to his friends about the intelligence and accomplishments of his other children without acknowledging me even if I was in the room. Eventually, there was a day when it all came to a point that pierced me to my core, wounding me for life. At that moment, *rejection* became my identity.

Merriam-Webster's dictionary defines Reject - as a transitive verb which means to refuse to accept, consider, submit to, or take for some purpose or use. It can also mean failing to show due affection or concern for someone. Rejection means the person or thing set aside is inferior in quality. This definition explains why rejection makes us feel inadequate when in all reality, we are more than enough. Unfortunately, the people, places, or things we're interacting with may not have known how to receive us in all of our glory, so to speak.

Now allow me to paint the picture. It was a beautiful fall day in 1989. It was my freshman year of college and only six months after my father made his last child support payment. I called him and asked for $150 to buy books, and he quickly replied, "I don't have any money. I already have a family." Since I never really asked for anything, I was stunned. His words were a gut punch I wasn't expecting. My response was sweet and simple. "F* you! It takes more than sperm to be a father!" I hung up and never called him again. Little did I realize how that pivotal moment would impact the rest of my life and so many of my choices in the coming years. Although he didn't say the word, the result was clear. I felt *rejected* by the man who helped create me. What hurt the most was him not acknowledging me as his child, his firstborn. I was no longer relevant because he remarried and had other children.

My father wasn't the first, and wouldn't be the last, person who refused to accept me for me. Although my mother showed great affection and concern, it was always clear she wanted me to be someone else. She told me on a few occasions that I wasn't feminine enough because I was a tomboy,

I was too timid, I didn't dress well, or in a way that flattered my figure, and so on. This was just the beginning of relationship after relationship, where who I was didn't work for them. Frequently I placed myself in situations where I would be rejected again and again, especially in connection with men who were emotionally and/or relationally unavailable. I needed to set myself aside and be who they wanted me to be since they loved me and had my best interests at heart.

In my twenties, I didn't date much at all. There were a couple of guys I was interested in, but nothing serious until my first marriage. This marriage filled a void when I felt like it was now or never. My first husband and I met and married within a few months of knowing each other. Our marriage lasted seven years, and I learned a lot about myself during that season of my life. To my surprise, I developed a greater level of endurance and resilience. This was tested the day I came home to find my husband and his belongings were gone. Initially, I was shocked and a little angry. I knew we weren't meant to be together, yet I didn't have the strength or courage to walk away. Now that the marriage was over, I was emotionally and spiritually broken, but also relieved. One week later, I left Michigan on my way back to Georgia. The car I drove back home had to be returned to its previous owner because I couldn't make the payments. I was broke and jobless, and all I had left were a few minor possessions, including my clothes. This was one of the darkest moments in my life. My worst nightmare had become a reality. I was angry, bitter, rejected, alone, and dreading the return to Georgia. I even contemplated suicide to avoid returning home to live with my mother.

In isolation, I would deal with hurts and pains from my past. For the first couple of years, I did nothing, but wallow in my pain and anger. The few times I shared my story, the pain stung as if the incident just happened yesterday. Little did I comprehend how swallowing all that pain, frustration, and anger had created a stone fortress around my heart. Eventually, a friend encouraged me to confront my feelings so I could work toward resolution and recovery. Prayer, Bible study, and application of lessons on forgiveness helped me move forward. Throughout those dark times, journaling saved me. When there was no human I could trust with my feelings, my written prayers to God were all I had. In this critical state of being, I would soon recognize there was a deeply desperate longing for love and acceptance. Things in my life were shifting, and I began diligently seeking to be *chosen* by God, or anyone who seemed to accept me for who I was. I wanted to be seen, heard, known, and loved in all my quirky greatness. Unfortunately, no matter what I did, I continued to be rejected because I kept putting myself in unfavorable situations.

Although my personal relationships were failing, my work relationships were thriving. My work world *seemed* safe and accepting of me. This was one of the few places I could truly be me. It was where my personality, talents, quirkiness, and everything good about me could shine without apology! Even when there was no recognition for my accomplishments, the interactions and lasting impressions I made on my co-workers gave me the personal validation I sought. As I often said, "The work me is the real me. You can take it or leave it." That version of me was confident and self-assured, especially as I became more skilled in key job duties such as administrating, facilitating, and auditing. Until that dreadful week in March 2022 when my self-image was demolished, which pierced me to the depths of my soul! Let me explain. I recently changed jobs, going from an engineering consulting firm to a product manufacturing plant. I was well-versed in quality auditing either way. That was my thought until we almost failed our annual system audit. Failing the audit would have significant financial ramifications for the company which could easily cause me to lose my new job. How was this possible? The audit guru I imagined myself to be didn't actually exist. I had been humiliated and humbled in an area where I felt extremely confident. As the saying goes, "Pride goes before destruction, a haughty spirit before the fall" (see Proverbs 16:18 NIV). I had a newfound appreciation for Humpty Dumpty! I, too, had fallen to the proverbial ground and now my work life felt shattered. Although no one could put Humpty back together again, I knew God would heal and make me whole in HIS own time. This gave me hope to pick up my broken pieces and keep moving forward.

Fast forward and it's now the first weekend in June 2023. I was at a spiritual retreat, and we were asked to pick a stone representing a critical event when everything changed. I looked for a stone with jagged and smooth edges. These contrasts in the stone represent the pain still present along with the smooth parts of me worn down over time by the trials and tribulations of life. Once we picked our stone, we had to stand before the group to tell our story. The emotional and physical pains throughout my past suddenly came flooding back. I was speechless as the tears filled my eyes before rolling down my cheeks. Although I always felt loved, the more dominant feeling was being *rejected* by those who should've loved me the most. My mother, father, family, and a few friends wanted me to be someone other than who I was or who God created me to be. They gladly told me how or why I wasn't due affection or care at various points. It was because I was gullible, too sensitive, couldn't take being corrected, and my words were never the right ones. At every turn, who I was, wasn't good enough. I was repeatedly dismissed, and no matter what changes I made, it still wasn't the right choice. After sharing our stories, we had a chance during a later session to leave our stones at the altar before God and to be prayed over. I gladly left my stone and what it represented at the altar that day.

Since early 2020, I've searched for my true identity in Christ, trying to connect intimately with God. I had an understanding in my mind, but that understanding wasn't connecting with my heart. I couldn't *feel* God's love for me. Slowly but surely, God started revealing Himself and His love to me as time progressed. Before the retreat, a friend suggested I read the book *Redeeming Love* by Francine Rivers. He felt it would help me understand and embrace God's love for me. I started reading but lacked the enthusiasm my friend had expected because I wasn't fully grasping the meaning and depth of the novel. It wasn't until after reading the book's summary that I came to a clearer and more personal understanding of God's redeeming love. Absolutely amazing! Despite my past missteps, repeated mistakes, and occasional resistance to His call, God was still right there again and again, helping me overcome the harmful things in my life. Hallelujah! Where others have set me aside as some thing of lesser value, God continues showing me I am worthy of His affection and care!

During the last year, God allowed several people to cross my path and speak to me about various aspects of my new identity. I was in awe of these prophetic words. I took each of them in like a cool sweet drink on a hot summer day! I believed and received each word, and then I thanked God for pouring into me in such a beautiful way. I was being filled despite the stones surrounding my heart. I made a list so I wouldn't soon forget those beautiful words. The most profound word, the word repeatedly shared with me, was *chosen*. Interestingly enough, "Chosen" was a name I picked for myself a few years ago after I started this journey. Yet, I hadn't considered or fully embraced its meaning until now.

This is where the transformation truly begins, where my name changes from rejected to redeemed and ultimately to *"Chosen"*!

Below is a detailed definition of the word from Merriam Webster's dictionary. Please read it a few times and think about what it means.

Chosen [*ˈCHōzn] - *is a past participle of the verb "choose" (the opposite of reject) and an adjective that means "having been selected as the best or most appropriate." It can also mean "one who is the object of choice or of divine favor: an elect person."

In God's eyes, I was selected as the best or most appropriate, the object of choice or divine favor! Despite everything I had believed about myself, God will forever choose me!

As we all know, being chosen has its privileges! At some point in life, we all want to be chosen by someone or for something.

What privileges do you associate with being chosen? Do you believe those privileges could apply to you?

Is God speaking to you? Is He calling you out of darkness into His wonderful light? Are you running in the opposite direction, hiding behind a tree, or throwing a tantrum like I was? Stop! Look! Listen! God has chosen *you*! He wants your heart! The road is not easy, but the reward of following His path is beyond anything you can imagine (see Ephesians 3:20-21 NIV). I'm only beginning to glimpse what's to come, and it's amazing!

Please join us on this journey of healing and transformation as we walk with our gracious heavenly Father. It's a decision you won't regret!

Food for Thought: What negative or demeaning name(s) have you been given that you need to let go of? What name has God given you that you seriously need to embrace? What steps must you take to identify and embrace your new God given name? For me journaling, writing this chapter, prayer, Bible study, and being in a community with like-minded people has made it possible for me to embrace my new identity and my calling. Please consider taking time to journal; to write your story so you can begin to experience The Transformative Power of a Name!

Feel free to follow me on social media as I chronicle my transformational journey of embracing my new identity as one of God's chosen. I'm not there yet, but I will get there because God is guiding my steps along the right path. To help me embrace my new identity, I've added speaking positive affirmations to my routine. It is written that life and death are in the power of the tongue. So I encourage you to choose life by speaking positively about yourself and working to become who God created you to be. Be blessed. See Proverbs 18:21 and Deuteronomy 30:19-20.

REFLECTIONS

A DAUGHTER REDEEMED HER NAME

Dr. Griselda T. Martínez

January 29, 1995, just a few hours after my oldest sister's 23rd birthday, marked the saddest day of my 16-year-old life. My mother, who was only fifty-two years old, died at the hospital after being admitted and released a few times that week. This moment would negatively define the next twenty-seven years of my life until the reconnection to my mother's love and the materialization of a personal relationship with God that led to deep healing of what I called the "famine" of a lost mother.

I remember walking into the hospital room. There were a few beds on both sides of that cold, white tile-covered room, with long curtains dividing spaces and compartmentalizing the deep struggles in that room. And then, in that horrible, uncomfortable hospital bed, under the harsh white sheet, was her body. My mother's body was just there, resting, with no life in it; her eyes were closed. It was my first time seeing a body with no life. As an impulse, I went to hold her hand, expecting the same in return—a touch filled with love that only she could do and often did. There was no response; something had changed. For the first time, my mother did not love me back. At that precise moment, my life and that of my four siblings was about to change in ways I would have never imagined. I have replayed this precise moment thousands of times over the last 28 years.

Frankly, I don't remember much about what happened in the next few days or weeks. I only remember the aftermath of this awful life-changing event. The glue that tied us together as a family and who created a home for her children was no longer there. She was also an extraordinary house-hold administrator and the best chef, feeding the five hungry mouths of her children. Never a hungry day with my mother.

That moment felt so opposite to the vivid memories of my life prior to my mother's death, where love, protection, and food were bountiful. Rapidly, I had replaced my loving name as a daughter with the stinging name of an orphan, filled with sorrow, a tremendous sense of loss, and a lack of belongingness.

Despite it all, life continued. We had to keep going even when we did not know where we were going. There, without the option to grieve, a new chapter titled "The Famine of Motherhood" began. Without my mother, I was like a leaf that had fallen from a tree, detached from its source of nutrients, on the ground, deemed to dry and perish. The person who taught me how to choose joy amid life's complexities was no longer with me.

Without her, though, all that I enjoyed prior became a latent presence. Years passed, and the consciousness of missing her faded away. However, the results of her absence filled an entire compartment of my being. That space was occupied by loneliness, sadness, and a lack of deep peace alongside hidden rage and resentment for those responsible for my abandonment – God and my mother herself. No way God existed! If there was a God, why had my mother died, leaving me in that dark place? Even more so, why did she leave me? Because of that, I avoided everything my mother taught me about God and His power as I continued my life. This unsettlement of mine showed up differently in the years that followed.

During my young adulthood, I was a happy person with laughs and smiles. Underneath that, though, there was a constant fear of losing a loved one and, tied to that, a sense of desperation to do anything to prevent it. In big moments, when happiness and joy would be expected as overflowing emotions, I reminisce melancholy. When this dark cloud was present, it dimmed the past and present blessings as I had been enveloped in life's benevolence with the love and support of the family I still had on Earth throughout my life. I diligently carried out my adulting responsibilities while embarking on exploring the world. My life was filled with undeserved favors, including my finances.

In later years, however, my finances took a turn, and a financial crisis knocked on my door at the exact time as the global recession—I found myself jobless without prospects on the horizon. The financial issues catalyzed a personal crisis, and opportunities for my future seemed stripped. It was such my desperation for a solution and the need to get out of that sinister place that I was forced to look up; the answer was not around me. Soon after, I remember going to church on a Sunday. During worship, I could not help but go to my knees and cry. I cried as I had not cried, maybe ever before. For the first time in my adult life, I sought God – or maybe I had finally answered God's multiple phone calls and telegrams. Suddenly, deep mourning surfaced and overflowed my soul. Then, a miracle happened; profound peace and joy came to me. It was the first time I remember being at peace despite my mother not being there.

Regardless of that experience bringing peace and joy, I got busy and distracted with living life with my career at its core. Without intentional work to nurture my connection with God, I detached. Yet, it was like a swapping transaction–peace or famine–as if the flowing waters of peace I had experienced had taken over the space where famine was. Without it, it yielded to its alternative as in previous times. My mother's passing continued to be a life marker. I remember turning 32 and reflecting that I had been without my mother for half my life.

Fast forward to the age of 42, as an accomplished professional, an emotional crisis was triggered by my working life. I felt hopeless, and while I desired a brighter future, I despised humanity and its faulty character. That situation resulted in the famine resurfacing in the strongest form I had yet experienced. Even though I knew I was in a crisis, I was oblivious to a larger underlying issue.

How could I not realize that the heart pain of all these years was all connected to missing my mother? Well, it is simple. I was busy dealing with the symptoms. Also, as I grew older, I had forgotten what it was to have my mother with me. As difficult as it was, I had to acknowledge that my hardship derived from when I had grabbed onto the label of an orphan and all that came with it. I wanted to remember my mother with joy rather than suffering. Even in her absence, my mother had a remarkable impact on my life. Yet, during all these years, her memory triggered so much hurt. For the first time, I remember not wanting to hurt anymore.

I needed to revert the effects of allowing anguish to be my normal; I required deliverance.

God had returned to get me from where I was once again. I knew that to leave that obscure place, I needed to dig through the buried and archived ache tied to my famine of motherhood. I sought a counselor to help me. She told me that through our work, I was going to be able to think about my mother without agony. I did not believe it. More so, that statement brought fear to my heart. I did not want to forget my mother. Was I betraying the loyalty to my mother's memories by removing the hurt?

My counselor guided me through much work, including challenging myself to write a letter to my mother saying goodbye. She asked me to write everything I needed to tell her, including my misery and resentment towards her and God. Why was she not there to share with me stories of her childhood, of how she had become the woman she was, to guide me as I became a woman, to cheer for me when things went wrong, to restore our family, and, lastly, to love me?

It was December 9, 2021, when after fighting the assignment for close to six months, I started the letter. I asked my mother straight up why she had wanted to leave. Did she decide to die? Did she know it was going to happen that soon? As I wrote this letter, my heartbeat was racing, my breathing was short, and tears inundated my soul.

Then, the next trial was to read this letter out loud, requested by my counselor. Why did I need to do it? It already had been distressing enough to write it. When I read it, I wept during the entire recital. As if this had not been sufficient mourning, the next instruction was to write a returning letter from my mother. After some additional pushback, on January 11, 2022, I started writing. As I wrote, a deep sorrow wrapped around me. I can't describe how much I wanted to put everything behind me. Yet, after a few months, my counselor asked if I was ready to read that letter to myself. The answer was no, but the potential to stop the hurt was at stake.

On July 21, 2022, I read the second letter out loud. To my surprise, it read truly as a letter from my mother. Miraculously, all her love and kindness for me were contained in it. The name orphan was fading away as her love wrapped around me through those written words. She responded to every challenging question I had posed to her a few months earlier. She called me her little daughter; she reminded me how much she loved me and how proud she was of me. She assured me I was the best daughter I could have ever been. She reminded me of our moments together, filled with joy, laughter, and overflowing love. I was told to enjoy and treasure the memories – few or otherwise – with the certainty that they had happened.

She asked me to forgive her for having left so soon. This brought peace to me as that huge question had been addressed. She reminded me that God's promises and grace would reach and protect me all my life, as she had prayed relentlessly during her time on Earth. She released me from the remorse of leaving my home country. She thanked God for my husband's life and said that with certainty, through my stories, he knew how much I loved her. She told me to be proud of the woman I had become. She encouraged me not to allow the things that I was not to define me. These words were like an oasis of fresh spring water in the desert, slowly canceling the title of an orphan. Instead, I was reminded I was my mother's daughter, and her love was reaching over.

The anger and spitefulness tied to orphanhood started transforming into gratefulness. God reminded me that my mother had been revived from dying 13 years prior to her final passing. With that, I received a second chance to have her a bit longer. My reproach of why only 16 years vanished and my heart was filled with thankfulness. I was holding on tight to what I thought was the last piece of my mother in me while ignoring that my mere presence, at that moment, represented who she had been.

I was fully conscious while experiencing those wounds, and their symptoms were being repaired. As this redemption process continued, a deep appreciation took over my heart for who my mother had been. I was exposed to her commitment to being the best mother she could have been as she held tight to her faith to enable her to do so. She provided, guided, and taught her children about miraculous provision and protection through example and out of faith in her God. The joy of understanding her devotion to being my mother, our mother, above everything else, overflowed my mind and heart. Through her actions, my mother demonstrated that she understood purpose and legacy. In that, God was showing me that my mother's purpose on Earth had been achieved, and I, at that moment, was evidence of it.

Then, I remembered a wise woman telling me, "Grief is love without a place to go." My grief was healed, making space for something else. And this love, once lost, needed to find a new place. But what could replace such a chamber in my heart, and where could all this love go? I was about to be filled with the deepest drive to seek my divinely designed purpose while living life to its intended fullest. I then understood that my mother had been bold and intentional in living her purpose, and I needed to follow in her footsteps.

If you related to anything captured in this story–loss, grief, and crisis – this is for you. We may continue our walks, pretending nothing needs to be addressed. Yet, when those still moments come, you and I know the aches of those unresolved wounds and hurts. We may keep going in life, surviving, numbing, and distracting ourselves while life passes before our eyes. We may keep taking ownership of those false names we picked up along the way and out of life's circumstances. We may be tricked into thinking that this place of ache is for us to stay. I have now learned that if we are willing, and allow it for ourselves, pain has an expiration date for healing to follow. Likewise, I stand in the certainty that pain does not define me, my identity, or my destiny. And the same applies to you.

If this story of grace, healing, and restoration had not been enough, on September 22, 2022, in a seemingly random conversation, I received an even bigger name. God called me His creation, His masterpiece. Further than that, He called me his daughter. My mother always told us that education was the only thing she would leave us as our heritage, and she did. Yet, she left us with an even bigger legacy, the best one anyone can ask for - our faith and the seeds planted by her unstoppable prayers. A faith that moves mountains, one that brings a peace that surpasses any understanding, and a love that exceeds anything else we may know. Because of my mother's prayers, goodness, mercy, and unfailing love have been with each one of her children. And I know they will reach the children of these children and the generations to come. For the skeptical ones out there, I know that pain is part of life. But I also now know that so is healing because a life filled with purpose, peace, and joy is on the other side. While I still miss my mother, an orphan is no longer my name. My daughterhood has been redeemed.

REFLECTIONS

BECOMING HAPPINESS

Felicity Blunt, MA, LPC S, NCC

Melancholy. That's how a friend once described me who had known me for over a decade. She made a profound statement about my personality and character, and in that moment, I was livid! How dare she question how I expressed my hurt? The hurt stemmed from being sexually and verbally abused as a child. She had no clue about the depths of darkness I have faced. At the moment, my indignation was about what I perceived as callousness and insensitivity. This was not the first time this particular friend made a negative judgment about me based on something I shared. Yet, as I reflect on this memory, it took me decades to realize I had been wearing the residue of what I had been through, and it impacted the quality of my life and relationships. The true culprit of my disdain was that this film was preventing me from living up to my name, Felicity, which means Happiness.

I wasn't striving for attention, but seeking some support and validation for what I had experienced. From losing my innocence due to molestation starting at age six, being bullied from elementary through middle school, attempting to take my life at 14, witnessing the demise of my parent's marriage, being verbally abused and disowned by my father at 15, and entering into a caregiver role in my teens that escalated until the end of my 30's. I was broken and desperately longed for anyone to acknowledge what I had lived through and offer some glue to help me put the pieces of my fragmented heart back together.

I have grappled with my name and its meaning for most of my life. Since I can remember, I have been in conflict with who I felt like and who I was named to be. Even when I inquired about the inspiration behind my name, my mother would smile, and explain how being pregnant with me was the happiest time in her life. I often wondered how to live up to such a lofty persona. How could I be an example of happiness, when my most prevalent emotions were fear, loneliness, sadness, confusion, and shame? Things were sweet before I could fully pronounce and correctly spell my name, however, my secure world became a danger zone in the blink of an eye.

Imposter Syndrome is real. From ages 6-16, everything about me on the outside looked intact by my grades, accolades, and compliance. I knew how to sweep a school awards ceremony year after year, and teachers raved about my conscientiousness. On the inside, a storm was raging as I tucked away each violation of my mind and body. I constantly felt I was living a double life, and it was difficult to keep up appearances. I didn't have the words to describe what was happening because I repressed every incident. All I was left with were the internal scars that whispered to me in the dark that the world was not a safe place.

As I sat in my first-grade class, I made my first big decision to disassociate myself from the pressure of being happy when I wasn't. In her zeal, my teacher had a cute symbol for everyone's first name; mine was the sun. I looked at that smiling sun and knew that image could not be further from who I was so I opted to be known by my middle name. This name, Neicole, was so common, it allowed me to blend in without any external pressure. I wanted to vanish far away because shame caused me to want to hide. I managed to get all the way to my first year of high school without being formally known as

Felicity. Unconsciously, it became important for me to escape so I turned to food to comfort my fear of feeling unprotected. I lost myself in books where I could avoid reality and pretend to be whoever I wanted other than me. My plan to remain distant from being bright and shiny seemed to work until it didn't.

My teen years brought out a level of rebellion towards authority that I began to exercise only when no one was watching. All that mattered was that I appeared to be a good girl. The one who helped out at home and caused no embarrassment in public; this is what I believed was expected of me. Never mind the disappearance of my self-esteem and self-respect, my main focus was to present well in front of others which was a confusing and miserable existence. One I attempted to end abruptly, but there was another plan for my life I had yet to discover. A plan of redemption that would lead to me entering my healing journey, and then becoming an advocate, supporter, and cheerleader for those walking through the darkness.

As life continued to unravel as a teenager, my parents separated, and I chose to relocate with my very ill mother and two younger siblings. They needed me. I was sure of this, way more than my father, who didn't even seem to like me. This sentiment became real as he expressed his pain. The words he spoke reduced me to nothing. I was extremely naive and had no clue how hurt is passed from generation to generation until someone interrupted the cycle. All I knew was that I felt lost. I decided to no longer go by my middle name in an attempt to gain some semblance of control. I wanted to detach from all the bitterness associated with those years of my life. I wanted to somehow erase everything negatively tied to Neicole. I wanted to try to be happy so I adopted Felicity. I officially asked family and friends to refrain from calling me Neicole and refer to me as Felicity. I put forth great efforts to live up to this name, much to my dismay. The name was mine on paper, but I had not forged a healthy connection with its meaning. I had yet to acquire the tools and develop the skills to help me step into who I was created to be.

Many years ensued and my actions continued to not match the definition of my name. I engaged in risky, self-sabotaging behaviors and toxic relationships as a way to numb my pain. I did not have a clear sense of who I was which made it easy to lose myself in anything.

I had no idea at the time that what was driving my behaviors was a deep need to be seen and truly understood.

How could I get others to see me when I couldn't see myself? I was on a path of self-destruction. When I hit a new low and lost all hope, I was introduced to Jesus. I had vaguely heard about Jesus when I would occasionally visit the church with relatives or friends, but I had not formally met Him. Once I did, my life was forever changed. I was extremely excited about this new chapter, yet even as I developed a relationship with God and experienced seasons of bliss, the struggle to be "happy" continued.

I learned about my Heavenly Father, yet my relationship with my biological father was tumultuous. I soon understood the magnitude of the intersection of these two patriarchal figures in my life and how each shaped who I was and who I was becoming.

Each level of distress revealed another crack in my foundation, and I dived deeper into the Bible for clarity and began counseling to aid in the healing process. This was a game-changer on my path of self-discovery and many truths related to childhood trauma were revealed to me in the safety of a therapeutic environment.

As I struggled with the wounds of my past, the difficulty of seeing myself as happy persisted. I wanted to blame someone, and found fault in many, including God, at times. I still struggled with my relationship with God because I was still working out kinks with my earthly father. I had to identify and confront false narratives that plagued my mind about who I was. I thought my worth was based only on what I could offer others. I had trust issues, an unhealthy view of intimacy, and had not truly discovered how to accept and love myself the way God had intended.

How could I love others adequately if I couldn't love myself?

I feared the judgment of others, so I tried to be perfect by being a people-pleaser and a conflict-avoider. These behaviors were signs of a dangerously distorted perception of love and relationships. I loved God on the surface, yet had difficulty fully trusting and embracing His plan because my belief about my worth was flawed.

As I grew in my knowledge of a spiritual enemy working overtime to keep me frustrated and confused about my identity, purpose, and calling, I could hear my mother saying, "I wish you could see yourself the way God sees you". Throughout my life, she planted seeds to help me believe in who God created me to be. She was my best friend, the one person in this world I knew loved and believed in me. As I held her hand as she lay in a coma, days before her passing, I desperately needed validation of God's plan for my life.

I could feel the confidence she gave me slipping away, and I feared how I would carry on without her building me up. I soon learned she had been the mouthpiece for God all along. Although she had been nonverbal and unresponsive for weeks, this day, she responded to my inquiries by smiling and squeezing my hand. Whenever I asked a specific question about my future, she gently and lovingly offered the "yes" I needed to know everything would be alright. As I relished those final days with her I saw God's plan of reconciliation slowly unfold.

By this time, I had done significant spiritual and clinical work regarding my relationship with my father, and we were in a good place. We had a mutual respect for one another, which had evolved over the years to him becoming one of my favorite people in the world. In those sweet and agonizing moments with my mother, God used me to connect her and my father for a final resolution call hours before her death, and then she was gone.

In that instance, I saw both my parents not as the people who gave me life; but just as humans doing their best to figure out the meaning of their lives. I had to be stripped of everything I thought contributed to my identity to allow His message to permeate my mind and heart in a pure, unfiltered way. This spark ignited the possibility of an alternate perception of myself, yet this bliss would be slightly delayed.

Initially, the grieving process had me contemplating a name change, much like Naomi (Ruth 1:20-21). Grief is a well, and I am grateful I had God's Word and trusted confidantes to draw me out when I was drowning. The days and nights seemed endless, and I just remember being a shell of a person. I moved through life physically but was somewhere else mentally and emotionally. This went on for years because once my mother died, I finally felt I had the permission to grieve all other losses I had previously experienced, like the loss of my childhood. Learning to grieve healthily was an integral part of my journey, and it positioned me to hear God's prompting to start living up to my name.

On the other side of grief's intensity, I entered a season of preparation, then transformation. This consisted of more solitude than I had ever experienced. The solitude provided time to invest in myself spiritually, emotionally, mentally, and physically. I could hear my mother's voice and knew God was aligning me with His will. As my self-awareness grew, I took a huge leap of faith and decided to relocate. It became apparent that I was too familiar with my surroundings and needed to become uncomfortable to grow. I was reminded of all of the kneading and molding I did with Play Doh as a child to get the desired shape and results. As God's masterpiece, I willingly surrendered to being stretched and molded; my mindset was the first thing that needed re-adjusting.

I began to truly see myself differently. I began to see who God was calling me to be. He even gave me visions of myself at various stages of progression. In this season of transformation, God instructed me to come out of hiding, which meant that the old me had to die in order to give life to the new me starting to emerge. I was creating a bridge between who I was and who I was created to be, which was the strengthening of my faith, and dependence on the power of The Holy Spirit as my Ultimate Comforter.

During this time of intimacy with God, I have grown in the fruit of His Spirit: peace, love, patience, self-control, kindness, gentleness, faithfulness, goodness, and joy. (Galatians 5:22-23) I had experienced moments of happiness before this, but this encounter was entirely new. This was not based on emotion or circumstances; it was strictly based on my belief in who God is and what He promised for my life. He promised to 'never leave or forsake me' (Deuteronomy 31:6). With this and many other promises in mind, my vision had never been clearer. God had not abandoned me or His plan for my life. He took what was meant for my demise and weaved it into my story of restoration.

I now reclaim and entirely embrace my God-given name, Felicity. Living up to this name is not a destination, but a journey. The more I lean into my name, the more I feel myself becoming more authentically who I am supposed to be. Multiple people have told me recently how much my name fits me because happiness exudes from me!

The enemy used the roadblocks of my past to derail me from His vision for me. The vision that was also given to my mother when she named me. Walking in destiny gives me hope that the pain of my past is not wasted. Out of heartache grew a deep passion to love and be present with people.

What roadblocks have been used in your life to cause detours from your true identity? How and where have you drifted in search of your life's meaning?

What are you uniquely designed to do based on your personal life experiences?

What signs have you been minimizing or ignoring that have been put in place to get you back on the path originally set?

Who or what do you need to be reconciled with to live the life you were uniquely designed for?

Finally, who will you meet if you choose faith over fear; and hope instead of despair?

Denis Waitley stated, "Happiness cannot be traveled to, owned, earned, worn, or consumed. Happiness is the spiritual experience of living every minute with love, grace, and gratitude."

No matter what we face, our Creator knows our full potential and is waiting for our next decision to get us back in alignment with His intended course.

REFLECTIONS

DEFINING ME

RAVONDA B. ODEN

I'*m a do-gooder*! I give of myself to others and often neglect myself in the process. As a child, I observed my mother being a *good woman* to many others. A diagnosis of stenosis or narrowing of the spine and her inability to walk gave me a strong need to save my mother's life by doing good for her as she's done for countless others.

Sometimes, we may replace or repair the soles of our favorite pair of shoes to get more time wearing, enjoying, and feeling good in them. We repair things to make them better or last longer, but have you ever tried repairing or saving someone's life, especially your mother's? The real question that consumed my mind and body was, how can I save my mother from dying after my experience with the untimely death of my father and older brother? Will God allow me to 'do good' and save my mother's life after not knowing how to save my father's and brother's life?

In the spring of my sophomore year at Syracuse University, I went to visit my dad after my parents had been divorced a few years earlier. He called me into the room; the sun beamed across Tompkins Avenue like sunrays peeking through rain clouds after a summer rain shower. My dad sat with his shirt off and his leg thrown across the worn upholstered chair that my grandmother probably sat in with him when he was a baby. *What a beautiful image*, I thought.

He murmured, "Give me your hand and feel this." My father placed my hand on his left breast. He sat in silence and appeared to wait for my response. I said, "Daddy, there's something seriously wrong! Go to the doctor." As I managed to withdraw my hand from his hardened breast, our eyes locked with concern for what we both felt. As I monitored the time on the clock to meet friends, my dad and I continued to engage in small talk. I nibbled on peanut brittle stuck to the wrapper while he smoked his cigarette. As I left my dad, I rubbed his black curly hair. As a 19-year old, what was I to think?

Three months later, I got the call. The voice on the other end was calm but firm. It was my brother, Stan. He rarely called me when I was away at college. I knew something was wrong. He said, "Nikki, I need you to sit down. I replied, "Why?" He said, "Dad died!" I remained silent as the tears rolled down my face. My body was numb. I wondered, "Why did this happen? Losing my father at 19, as a sophomore in college, while pledging Delta Sigma Theta Sorority, Inc., was overwhelming. There was an emptiness in my heart knowing that my dad would not be able to attend my college graduation. I wondered why this was happening to us. I was a good daughter. I made the Dean's List as a freshman, adhered to my curfews, and never caused my parents stress. I wasn't ready to accept embarking on this milestone of adulthood without my father, but as each day passed, I had to keep going.

Three decades later, my phone rang again. This time it was my mother. She said, "Nikki, I think you should come to North Carolina now to see Stan!" My husband, Kelvin, and I relocated my brother from a nursing home in New York City to North Carolina, to be close to family. With his declining health, there was a familiar feeling that

I had experienced years earlier with my father. Once again, I asked, "How can I help save my brother's life? I visited him every chance I had. My mother used to say, "The worst thing in the world is for a parent to bury their child, and I never want that to be my story." The sun had set on our family prayer. Mom buried her only son, Stanley, a.k.a. 'Little Stan,' our only brother, on December 21, 2017. I surely miss my kindhearted, freckled, and dimpled-faced brother who always protected his sisters.

What does *doing good* really look like? How could I continue to do good for others when my own wellness was being compromised? Some days my heart would pound like a drum in my chest for no apparent reason. I was falling apart! How do I continue to be that *do-gooder* and share the best of myself when the worry of loved ones whose declining health and impending death continued to be the topic of my family's conversations?

Several years later, my mother would lose her balance while walking on the stairs, which resulted in a broken toe, and multiple bruises. The deterioration of her spine was the source of her imbalance. The nerve damage from seven spinal surgeries gave her more time to be mobile, however, I tried to keep prayer at the forefront of my thoughts throughout the day. I still worried anyway. My collection of thousands of family photos and videos told the visual and physical timeline of my mother's story of her fight to live. The question that got louder and clearer in my head was: *Will Mom become paralyzed*? A few years later, paralysis was no longer a possibility but our reality. She'd never use the 'P' word. She'd say, "I can't use my feet now, but I will. I'm walking out of here. I'm leaving this bed and walking right out of this bedroom!" I love her courage and her faith! These incidents forced me to focus more on the question, how can I save my mother's life?

Many conversations with earth angels and prayer warriors helped me to know I was enough and did what God wanted me to do with the time He gifted us. God knows my heart, and I no longer had to live in fear of the inevitable. Our days are numbered on this earth; only God knows! "Trust in the Lord with all your heart, and lean not on your own understanding; In all your ways acknowledge Him, and he shall direct your paths." NKJV Proverbs 3:5-7.

My entire life, I'd heard my mother's phone conversations. Her favorite pastime was connecting with family, friends, and former students. There were many days when she was talking on the phone and baking a cake from scratch, I'd hear her say, "She's a good girl. She's doing good." I knew she was referring to me because it felt natural to me to want to leave a situation or person in a better place than before. It was important to me to show God my heart every day and in every way.

My mother was a *good woman*. She once rescued her student's family, who was displaced by a tenement building fire at 2 a.m. on a school day. My mother, Sylvia E. Blount, gave of herself, and I, as a quiet child, often watched her counsel, protect, and defend many people by any means. I can still hear those words from the kitchen to the bedroom, "Stay out of grown folks' business," but it felt good to be helpful, kind, and loving to those around me. She modeled that for me throughout my life.

I was a *do-gooder* long before I realized it. Doing good was a driving force inside me. Imagine the difficulty of a *do-gooder* functioning amidst newly occurring anxiety, panic attacks, loss of appetite, hair loss, and the fear of the inevitable—my mother's death. Her slow decline over many years became more apparent. I needed to do something to keep her living in joy and find humor to distract her from her pain. I knew that my serious face while dancing silly would make her laugh until her side hurt. She'd always beg me to stop, but it made us both feel better. That was the good girl in me and in many others who brought her joy with a plethora of acts of kindness. I was living up to my name my entire life: a *good girl* who gives and goes the extra mile to make any situation better. Whatever the outcome, it is God's will.

I was finally able to truly process what Mom meant when she said, 'Let go and let God.' She prepared me for acceptance, understanding the true process of life's journey, and living with no regret. It is in my heart to make a positive difference, although my heart ached with the anticipated void in my life; living without her. I had to keep the faith. Letting go and letting God was the only answer to this tug-of-war in my spirit. I was desperate to save my mother, whom I loved and admired. She shaped me to be who I am today, and my burning desire to help her not worry was seen in my actions. My good deeds were a short-term fix for her, although carrying them out felt good. God was always in control and surely the only Fixer in the equation. I wasn't ready to accept the facts before me—my mother was dying, and I couldn't save her. But I had to get ready for the inevitable! I prayed, "God grant me the serenity to change the things I can, the courage to accept the things I cannot change, and the wisdom to know the difference." I continued to say that same prayer.

The need to do good has been a part of me since childhood and is nothing new. As a child, I'd protect a schoolmate from being teased, and as an adult, I continue to uplift others' spirits. I recently ran full speed escorting a blind man in Charlotte Airport to catch his flight before the gate closed. I'd buy groceries for the elderly person standing in line in front of me, pay rent for a young mother to avoid eviction weeks after giving birth, and build a new home for my mother to live in that absolutely improved her quality of life. The list goes on with good deeds for family and friends alike. I am at peace and live in joy because I gave my all and continue to live my life with purpose while paying homage to her legacy of service to others, and that makes my heart smile.

As I continue to grieve my mother's passing on January 28, 2023, I must also continue to live with a strong faith and display my gratitude for many wonderful blessings, especially the time He has granted us. I've learned to never question God but to accept His will. I will continue to be a *do-gooder* while keeping God in the forefront and in the driver's seat. I've realized that some things were never meant for me to fix, but just *to be* as I work to better align my life with God's word while getting to know myself in my aloneness. I will always find joy in the life cycle of births while also accepting the unavoidable seasons of death. Life requires doing *real work* in *real tim*e to prepare for death. The sweet memories of my mother's love for life, her transition, and the birth of my granddaughter Ariah, who met her great Nana six days before she took her last breath. Only God provided the gift of time for that moment to occur as I filmed their first introduction. He shares His gifts with me, and I must also accept them when He takes them back. Time was God's gift to us all. He gave me time to prepare for loss and create great memories of my mother's life as death drew nearer. I don't know how much time that either I, or my loved ones have left to live. As mom would say, "Everything is totally out of my hands. It's always in God's hands."

The Bible says, "These things I have spoken to you, that in Me you may have peace. In the world you will have tribulation; but be of good cheer, I have overcome the world." (John 16:33 NKJV). I cheerfully choose to be who I am, a *do-gooder* who shows that I care for others, and I care for myself while carrying forth my mother's legacy of love, kindness, and gratitude. My faith is growing stronger and deeper with each sunrise and sunset. I see more clearly how God has guided my life's path as I continue to do God's work—positively impacting others in my personal and professional lives, which gives me a greater sense of purpose. It brought me joy to say, "Mom, I got you!" For the past two years, when she could not walk, my worldly tasks were to keep her alive if possible and prevent her from becoming depressed again. I believed I could do just that. I fulfilled my need to be a blessing to her by sharing my God-given gifts. "Let us not become weary in doing good, for at the proper time, we will reap a harvest if we do not give up. Therefore, as we have the opportunity, let us do good to all people, especially those who belong to the family of believers." (Galatians 6:9-10 NIV).

Being a *do-gooder* has prepared me for my mother's transition to a spiritual being because I have harvested her love and am fulfilled knowing that she knew she was loved by many and that I did good. As they say in sports, "I left it all on the court." God has granted me the space in this place!

What name are you honoring in this space?

REFLECTIONS

THE BIRTH AND END OF ROMANTIC WOMAN

Erika D. Gould Brown

Romantic. It's one of those words that may mean different things to different people. So please allow me to clarify. Specifically, in my case, I refer to those of us who live with an idealized view of reality. Still unimpressed? Hard to see how anyone would see being a romantic as an issue. Such a harmless word. Or is it?

I was born with a birthmark on the top of my left knee. Time (and weight changes) have blurred its clarity a bit. But, the two concentric circles that touched in the middle were a familiar point of interest for me as a child. In my little opinion, I was certain that it was a butterfly on my knee.

I was eventually corrected. "It's not a butterfly. It's a bow," my mother informed me. "While I was pregnant with you, all I did was dream about little girls with bows in their hair. And you came out with a bow on your knee," she shared.

Either interpretation was special to me and was a sure indication of the *happily ever after* I was destined for. I didn't speak about it. I simply knew it in my bones. I was a little girl of the seventies, raised on anklet socks, ribbons, doll babies, and fairy tales. A *good* girl who didn't question but obeyed. I said *please* and *thank you* and never interrupted adults. I had determined that my *good* would pave the pathway to the future I had so often read about.

My parents read to me every night before bed. It was a fantastic show, all for me. Each character was always given a dynamic voice. They oozed with emotions as the characters traveled through their adventures. Every page came alive. I cannot overstate the wonder and amazement their performances ignited in me. Their talent and tireless devotion to reading to their child produced a ravenous reader. I devoured books. And my favorite literary food of choice was the fairy tale.

There was no way I could know, reading these familiar stories as a child, the depth of their impact on my understanding and expectations of life. Or the ways they would shape me. I didn't know that there were better, more helpful books that were a much better investment of time. There was no Google then. And I couldn't know by a few simple clicks on a keyboard that the definition of a fairy tale isn't just a children's story about magical and *imaginary b*eings and lands. That it isn't just *idealized* or extremely happy. I was easy pickings for the deception. Literal low-hanging fruit. Those stories were simply wonderful to me. They were so satisfying and seemed so *right*. But, the fairy tale is a *fabricated* story, especially one *intended to deceive.*

Marked for romantic greatness with my butterfly-bow birthmark, I was certain that I was part of a living, modern fairy tale. My parent's relationship became my baseline evidence. They checked off so many of the fairy tale "must- haves." My mother was beautiful. I would hear it all the time from friends. With awe, they would whisper, "Your mom is so pretty." I agreed. My dad was smart, tall, handsome, and fit. He worked hard and earned enough to allow my mother to be a stay-at-home mom and for me to be outfitted with plenty of books and toys.

They overcame hard obstacles to get where they were. As eldest children, both were treated more as servants than family. They survived their childhood rather than being raised. But they found each other. My mom was just fourteen when she and my dad, four years her senior, began to date. He married her when she was eighteen. He was finishing college; the first, in either family, to ever attend. Ten months later, after dreaming of little girls with bows in their hair, they had me. The *princess* with a butterfly-bow birthmark.

I adopted their relationship timeline as mine. I knew it was just a matter of time before my prince came. I looked forward to him courting me, to the romance I would experience, and to being cherished by the only love of my life. Their *plot* fed my romantic folly. Their story was my reassurance when I hit bumps in the road. I can only tell you these things now as I reflect back. At the time, I didn't understand my delusion. I had no idea how lost I was in the woods.

Romantics idealize love. We also idealize reality. Romance became my idol. The deception I lived under was subtle and pervasive. It kept me trapped and bound, while I barely noticed. It tethered me to a place and in a space that would never serve me or my greater purpose. Those fairy tales with their satisfying story lines, meant to entertain me, had instead entered my psyche and warped my worldview. I waited for my *prince* and my *happily ever after,* rather than to develop into the fullness of who I was created to be.

So as I grew, I mentally crammed and forced my circumstances into the form of my beloved genre. I soothed myself as I twisted my life's events into the plots of imaginary stories. The ever-growing list of endless chores that came with each additional brother and sister fit semi-perfectly into the idea of Cinderella being made to work hard before her big ball. The unfortunate angle at which my adult front teeth grew didn't make me the ridiculous "bucked tooth beaver" my classmates often hurled at me. I was simply the ugly duckling, destined to be a beautiful swan before I knew it. I knew the plot. *My day was coming.*

It was my unconscious internal mantra as I stayed obedient and sweet to all those around me. But reality brings pain, frustration, anger, and fear. And I largely ignored my real needs. I needed to know that I was wonderfully and fearfully made for a special purpose on this earth. Not to linger in waiting for someone else's story to happen to me. But, my spirit was entranced. Unresponsive to reality, I skipped over my insecurities and pain of feeling ugly and less than. I kept a sharp eye out for the hero who would come and make it all okay.

Fairytales have enemies like witches and dragons; not depression and low self-esteem like in real life. Again, I ignored my reality. According to my parent's timeline, I was due for my prince early in my high school career. I was primed and ready. I was smart and stayed at the top of my class. I was active and visible as a member of the school's student council, choir, and cheerleader squads. My heart was open and unguarded. I caught crushes like the tide comes in. For no other reason than they were *cute*. Time and time again, the gossip train would deliver the news that Erika likes <*insert name*>. And time and time again, the feelings were unrequited.

Singleness was not part of my plan. It had no part in my life's plot. Increasingly, my deception began to derail my development. Rather than researching schools and careers that my academic achievements supported, my focus turned inward to my deficiencies. There was no other conclusion to come to. I was inadequate. Unlovable. Simply not meant for the part or romantic lead in anyone's story.

I graduated high school with a full scholarship and an almost empty spirit. The romantic in me had placed the highest value of life on being a part of a loving couple. Something I had not experienced in high school at all. Now college loomed. I was heading into chapters I hadn't planned and didn't fit into my imaginary design. No love at first sight for me. And suddenly, during my first year of college, I was in an unexpected plot twist. My father left my mother.

As a romantic, the foundation of my life's philosophy had been built upon fragility. Fragile ideas and fragile circumstances I had little to no control over. And like dropping a phone; my father leaving my mother was a huge drop for me. I went to pick it up and move about my life. But, the screen has splintered. Cracks on top of cracks. I couldn't comprehend why I felt so broken by their separation. I've since been told that micro cracks happen with each fall. I just didn't see them. Until that one *perfect* drop. The stories I so loved never included the prince leaving the princess. My spirit shattered in ways that would take decades to fully understand. I mourned the loss of my precious family and my life's romantic role models, while at the same time, trying to navigate a new land. A land far away from the family I loved. A family traumatically transformed into something I didn't recognize.

I was adrift. Out in the world, single and seemingly unloved. And rather than destroy the romantic in me, the end of my parent's marriage emboldened me. I doubled down. Undeterred, I determined that I would find that prince. I soldiered on and stumbled through my college years and early twenties, always with the goal of finding true love. That was my solution to all that ailed me. I did little to nothing to be wise and guard my heart. And for that oversight, I was served a generous portion of heartache. I lied to myself. I minimized my mistakes with fairy tale sensibility. Maybe I had to kiss a few frogs.

Eventually, I found a handsome, funny, hard-working man. He asked me to be his wife. And I said yes!

One thing that intrigued and impressed me about him was something my family didn't do. He and his family were regular churchgoers. In true prince form, I had found someone who was going to help me to be *better*. My family respected God. We always said grace before eating. But, attending church was limited to the occasional Christmas or Easter holidays. I happily joined his small church and was baptized on a cold February Sunday.

Now, a different book entered the picture. I found there were many lessons to learn from it. Every Sunday, our congregation dove in. Slowly, I started to explore it on my own. Not a lot though. My *ever-after* was pretty full. I was, finally, a married woman working full-time as a school counselor. I tutored kids at an after-school program and took multiple weekly dance classes for fun. But, somehow, something felt wrong. I felt unfulfilled. Something was missing.

I remember it like it was yesterday. The first time I really cried out to God. I cried from that empty space within. I asked Him, "Is this all there is?" And I kept living. Not understanding that the romantic in me was about to be laid to rest.

God would answer my question. He would change my life forever. He would change my life for the better. But first, I had some storms that He needed to guide me through. Truth and reality would be the perfect poison to kill the romantic and set me free.

God's first intervention for me, came in the form of a pregnancy. *And* a diagnosis that would not permit me to live in the lie that my *prince* was a faithful partner.

This betrayal didn't just crack me. It shattered me. It shattered all trust. There was no *happily* in the diagnosis I had received. I could have easily died. I was certain that my heart had been annihilated. But for God! He had placed another heart inside of me. An innocent heart. A heart worth living for; even if mine was dead. That baby, my son, gave me purpose. He showed me how true love works. He was given to me, just in time to save me.

With God, I persevered and weathered many storms. Divorce was like a tornado; turning my life upside down. Then single motherhood brought more challenges. But both *plot twists* have resulted in the greatest rewards of my life. Today I live in gratitude. God was so gracious to me. I didn't mention God in my youth because He was an abstract concept then. A quick pause of acknowledgment before meals and before bed. Largely ignored other than that.

And yet, when I needed Him, He was there *like I had been faithful all my life*. He healed me before I gave birth. He let me parent a beautiful baby boy (now a beautiful young man). He strengthened me and *delivered* me from a marriage based on lies. He advised me to *forgive* when all I wanted to do was hate. He urges me to *learn* and grow to *give* to others.

Fairytales no longer deceive me. I am no mythical princess waiting for a prince. I am God's daughter-wonderfully and fearfully made. He crafted me for a purpose. And in part, that is to share my story and prayerfully help someone else avoid unnecessary heartache. I may not know what the next chapter of my story will bring; celebrations or sorrows, delight or defeat. But, with God, seeking Him, and leaning on Him, I can experience the fullness in life that I missed before. I can find contentment in my circumstances. I can heal and have hope today and in the days to come.

I look at my knee and see a butterfly. I believe it is a butterfly (and not a bow) even more today. Like a butterfly, I needed transformation. Or I could never be who I was meant to be. I could never do what I was meant to do. I needed transformation in my thinking. Transformation, in my understanding. Transformation in my heart. And just like the butterfly, I am unrecognizable from where I began. God is doing that for me. He is waiting, with open arms, for you as well.

Don't worry. Don't doubt. It's okay. You can come cracked, shattered, with your heart annihilated, even after kissing a ton of frogs. It doesn't matter how long you ignored Him or shunned Him, or even disbelieved. You are here today. And you are reading this invitation to change for the better.

As a child, I read and believed silly books with silly stories. I lived a large chunk of my life deceived, putting my faith into fantasy. Thinking that I was broken. Without value, unless some man professed his love. But after I learned what Book to put my hope in. I found out that I've been incredibly loved all along. Once I learned that the Book deserving of my faith and focus is really the Bible, I was given many things like peace and joy, forgiveness, and love.

James 1:17 NIV tells us, "Every good and perfect gift is from above, coming down from the Father…" To that, I can attest. Open your heart. Open your mind. And receive those gifts. Truly, our *happily ever after* lies in the love of God.

REFLECTIONS

ABOUT THE AUTHORS

CECILY COOPER

Cecily Cooper is a certified Transformational Life Coach, Speaker, and Author deeply dedicated to empowering women and youth by helping them to unlock their full potential. This work, her second publication, reflects her unwavering commitment to fulfilling the call of God on her life.

With a career spanning over two decades in education and leadership roles across private and public schools, Cecily has focused on nurturing her students' love for reading, writing, and critical thinking. Her professional journey extends into the corporate world, with notable positions at magazines like Essence and Emerge Magazine, as well as corporate sales at Xerox. Cecily seamlessly integrates her diverse experiences into all her professional pursuits.

A member of Delta Sigma Theta Sorority, Inc. since 1988, Cecily earned a Bachelor of Arts in English from Syracuse University and pursued further education, obtaining a dual Master's degree in Special and General Education from Touro College. In 2019, she received a post-Master's Certification in Administration and Supervision from Notre Dame of Maryland University. Cecily's true passion lies in coaching, mentoring, and empowering individuals to rebound from life's challenges, enabling them to regain their God-given impact, influence, and income.

Scan below to connect with Cecily.

SHANNON WALKER

Shannon Walker is a highly respected trainer and leader in the canine industry. Her understanding of canine instincts and natural abilities has been the corner- stone of her business, transforming dogs into disciplined family pets, invaluable partner for law enforcement, and life-altering service dogs for Veterans.

Inspired by her father's and twin sons' military service, and driven by her confidence in the human-canine bond, Shannon established a nonprofit organization that provides service dogs to Veterans with post-traumatic stress. Her commitment to American heroes and accomplishments in developing superior service dogs have earned her recognition from her peers, leading to her appointment as the head of the national ASDPMV serving the Veteran community.

Shannon's influence transcends her businesses as she shares her expertise through a free social media platform. With her remarkable accomplishments and steadfast commitment to helping others, Shannon Walker emerges as a true leader and influencer in the field.

Scan below to connect with Shannon.

DR. JUDINE BERLUS

Meet the remarkable, Dr. Judine Berlus, a multi-talented professional. Dr. Berlus is an astute entrepreneur, pharmacist, and real estate investor. She is a devoted wife, daughter, and mother; however, she is most accurately defined as an ambassador of the Gospel. With over 15 years as a pharmacist, Dr. Berlus boasts a wealth of knowledge. She holds a pivotal position as a senior pharmacist at the Food and Drug Administration, assessing risk evaluation and mitigation strategies for medications with serious adverse events.

Prior to the FDA, she spent more than a decade at CVS health where she served as a District Leader. In this role, she skillfully managed 13 locations, adeptly led a team of 340 employees, and masterminded a $150 million budget.

Dr. Berlus graduated magna cum laude with a Doctorate in Pharmacy from Palm Beach Atlantic University in 2008 and obtained her Master's in Public Health from Johns Hopkins University in 2013.

Scan below to connect with Dr. Judine.

DIANNE REID

Dianne Reid is a timely, evolutionary and transformational leader, speaker, coach and author. Through the written and spoken word, she unlocks destinies by delivering people from a place of self-doubt to a paradise of self-assurance. As Founder and CEO of Annelytics Anew, LLC and creator of the Confrontation of Calling, Dianne cultivates safe spaces and provides resources and coaching for leaders to contend for and confidently accept their callings. Her experiences in the educational, non-profit and corporate sectors have given her a unique skill set to create multi-generational content and workshops so people can process, heal, and be rooted in who they were created to be. In a world where many are in desperate search of identity, Dianne affirms that a person is never too young or old to confront and live out their calling. Her empathy, love and strength inspires others to not just survive but to thrive unapologetically.

Scan below to connect with Dianne.

SOPHIA K. TADE

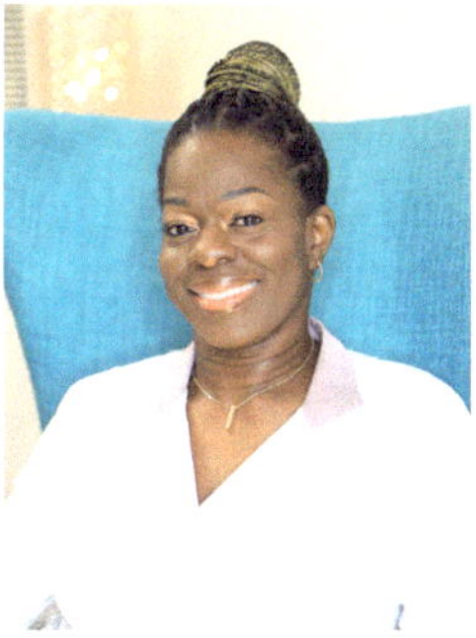

Sophia Tade is an accomplished business owner and natural healer. She is passionate about awakening the true healing power from within. Sofia interrupted a burgeoning career in talent management consulting to pursue her passion of holistic healing. She successfully brought her vision of owning a holistic spa to fruition, while working as a senior legal consultant for an international law firm. She is also a God-fearing disciple of the Lord and serves on the Women Leadership Development Institute and Cancer Care Ministry at her local church.

Sophia holds a Master of Science in Business Law and a postgraduate certificate in Instructional System Design. She is PMP certified, Hermann Brain Dominance Instrument (HBDI) Levels I and II Practitioner, and Certified Product Innovation Professional (CPIP) to cite a few. She is also a master esthetician, oncology-trained esthetician, and a functional nutrition counselor. She lives in Columbia MD with her daughter.

Connect with Sophia at:

https://buy.stripe.com/9AQfZk0mT5sD6YM3cc

BRITTANI WEGNER

Brittani Wegner is a certified transformational coach whose passion is to lead others to freedom through inner healing and connection to their true self. She does this by helping people break free from unhealthy cycles and patterns so they can live their life filled with peace, joy, and love.

Brittani's hunger to share this work with others is due to her own journey of inner healing where God helped her break free from unhealthy cycles and patterns of shame, judgment, and self-hatred. Brittani believes that it is because of her firm foundation in her faith that she is able to share the fruits of her own journey with you!

Scan below to connect with Brittani.

KEM S. KITCHEN

Walkemma (Kem) Scott Kitchen is a knowledgepreneur and the General Manager of K. Kitchen Enter- prises, LLC–A Speaking, Coaching and Consulting firm. Kem is a certified Transformational Speaker and Coach with a specialty in Grief Recovery and Mental Health. She has a B.S. degree in Chemical Engineering from Tuskegee University. Kem has worked over 28 years in the automotive industry where she held various engineering positions and obtained several quality system certifications. She currently works as a Quality Systems Manager.

Kem is a southern belle, born and raised in Georgia to a family of teachers. Therefore, education was always important. Kem was a curious child with a desire to write and teach. Her appreciation for thoughtful words, unexpected definitions and powerful mental imagery fueled a love for writing as her creative outlet. In her chapter, Kem shares some frustrations in her life and the joys of her transformation process.

Scan below to connect with Kem.

DR. GRISELDA MARTÍNEZ

Dr. Griselda Martínez Cereceres has journeyed through a mosaic of experiences shaping her perspective on life, love, and self-discovery. Griselda was born and raised in Parral, Chihuahua, Mexico. As a young adult, she immigrated to the United States for her education, where she decided to make it her home away from home. Her story sheds light on the power of boldness to seek healing as a passageway to find her divinely designed purpose. Her path to purpose includes a diverse 20-year career, including her roles as an economic development consultant, transformational business coach, speaker, and podcaster. Griselda is a Certified Transformational Coach and Speaker, a Certified Economic Developer, and holds a doctoral degree in economic development. She hopes her story incites those who have been through deep hurts and disappointments to fight for healing, find peace, and grow in gratefulness to live the life we were created to be.

Scan below to connect with Dr. Griselda.

FELICITY BLUNT, MA, LPC-S, NCC

Felicity Blunt is an entrepreneur and Licensed Therapist of Blunt Counseling & Consulting (AL), and Certified Transformational Coach and Speaker of The Blunt Approach. She has made it her life's work to support others on their paths to healing from trauma and is extremely passionate about assisting individuals with shedding baggage holding them back from living out their created destiny.

Felicity is devoted to her faith, family, and friends who are the foundation of her life. She is grateful to be on a journey of transformation and hopes to inspire others to do the defining work of discovering the best version of themselves. She aspires to leave a personal and professional legacy of love and light in the world.

Scan below to connect with Felicity.

@BWHOLE_22

RAVONDA B. ODEN

Ravonda Blount-Oden is an entrepreneur, real estate investor, co-owner of Brooklyniteapparel.com and an Assistant Principal at P.S. 75 in Manhattan. She authored Romare Bearden: Piecing Together a Masterpiece, an art unit of study for PBS McNeil Lehr Report. With over 30 years of experience, Ravonda advocates for using the arts to engage, edify and empower her students.

Her most rewarding accomplishments are: raising her amazing children, Nia and Taj and their growing families, her marriage to her high school sweetheart, Kelvin, and the opportunity to be part of this beloved community of brave women co-authors.

Ravonda is a graduate of Syracuse University: BFA in Interior Design; Brooklyn College: MS in Elementary Education; NYC Leadership Academy/Baruch College: Advanced Certificate in School Administration and Supervision.

She is a champion for children and believes in connecting to God's love to heal hurt, be inspired, and find peace in order to live in harmony.

Scan below to connect with Ravonda.

ERIKA D. GOULD BROWN

Erika D. Gould Brown is a career dance and fitness educator, counselor, certified life coach, personal trainer, premiere keynote speaker and CEO/ founder of EDGeee Services, LLC.

Erika, an enthusiastic lifelong learner, has committed herself to serve people and communities seeking paths to optimize their health and wellness.

Erika places emphasis on living joyfully with compassion and gratitude, all qualities that she infuses in life and work with others.

A native Delawarean, Erika received her B.S. in Psychology & English from the University of Delaware. She continued at U.D. to earn her Masters in Counseling. She discovered her love for dance and fitness while working part time as a professional cheerleader for the Philadelphia Eagles football team. This exposure to active living transformed her outlook and led her to begin teaching dance and fitness for two decades. Erika's greatest pride, however, lies in being a mother to her wonderful son, Kelley.

REFLECTIONS

Made in the USA
Columbia, SC
09 October 2024

43345496R00072